Miss-Adv

GUIDE TO

ULTIMATE EMPOWERMENT FOR WOMEN

Harness Your Power and Thrive in Every Area of Your Life

STEPHANIE BAILEY

Featuring: Jill Alman-Bernstein, Dr. Gretchen Bruno,
Christine Falcon-Daigle, Lori Frisher, Tanya Garner,
Lolita Guarin, Amber Jace, Pamela D. Jordan, Tiffany McBride,
Karen Rosenfeld Montgomery, Nolwazi Charmaine Nkosi,
Marion Noone, Anna Pereira, Billie Rinehart, Tara Rose Ritchie,
Denise Smith, Tanya Stokes, Jennifer Tasker,
Delores Tronco, Cynthia Webster, Georgia Wong

Miss Adventures Guide to Ultimate Empowerment For Women

Harness Your Power and Thrive in Every Area of Your Life

Stephanie Bailey

©Copyright 2022 Stephanie Bailey

Published by Brave Healer Productions

Paperback ISBN: 978-1-954047-78-5
eBook ISBN: 978-1-954047-77-8

Miss-Adventures

GUIDE TO

ULTIMATE EMPOWERMENT FOR WOMEN

HARNESS YOUR POWER AND THRIVE IN EVERY AREA OF YOUR LIFE

STEPHANIE BAILEY

FEATURING: JILL ALMAN-BERNSTEIN, DR. GRETCHEN BRUNO,
CHRISTINE FALCON-DAIGLE, LORI FRISHER, TANYA GARNER,
LOLITA GUARIN, AMBER JACE, PAMELA D. JORDAN, TIFFANY MCBRIDE,
KAREN ROSENFELD MONTGOMERY, NOLWAZI CHARMAINE NKOSI,
MARION NOONE, ANNA PEREIRA, BILLIE RINEHART, TARA ROSE RITCHIE,
DENISE SMITH, TANYA STOKES, JENNIFER TASKER,
DELORES TRONCO, CYNTHIA WEBSTER, GEORGIA WONG

DEDICATION

To all the women who have felt they were alone in their
circumstances, experiences and traumas.

To my childhood friend Karen Sole-Dwyer who inspired this book.

To God for guiding me every step of this journey to bring this book
to fruition.

DISCLAIMER

This book offers health and wellness information and is designed for educational purposes only. You should not rely on this information as a substitute for, nor does it replace professional medical advice, diagnosis, or treatment. If you have any concerns or questions about your physical or mental/emotional health, you should always consult with a physician or other healthcare professional. Do not disregard, avoid, or delay obtaining medical or health-related advice from your healthcare professional because of something you may have read here. The use of any information provided in this book is solely at your own risk.

Developments in medical research may impact the health, fitness, and nutritional advice that appears here. No assurances can be given that the information contained in this book will always include the most relevant findings or developments with respect to the particular material.

Having said all that, know that the experts here have shared their tools, practices, and knowledge with you with a sincere and generous intent to assist you on your health and wellness journey. Please contact them with any questions you may have about the techniques or information they provided. They will be happy to assist you further!

TABLE OF CONTENTS

INTRODUCTION

"If one person knows she is not alone, she is empowered."

~ Dr. Maya Angelou

"I'm adopted," my friend Karen blurted out to me in fourth grade.

What?! No way! Am I hearing her correctly? I squealed inside as my heart started beating faster, the corners of my mouth widened bigger then Cheshire Cat, and my eyes became so enlarged—I thought they would fall out of their sockets. I remember having this same feeling on Christmas day when I opened up my oversized Barbie doll at age six.

Yes! Finally, my wish of finding someone like me came true. This news, for me, was even better than the giant Barbie doll. As I took a deep breath, my shoulders relaxed, and my back became less tense; I no longer felt like an unwanted freak of nature or the only one whose parents didn't want them. Although I know now that wasn't true; however, when I was younger, I felt this deep inside.

Have you ever gone through an illness, break-up, or traumatic experience? Have you dated someone who then ghosted you, making you feel as if you could've, would've, done something differently—racking your brain and dissecting your entire experience with a fine-tooth comb? I have. This feeling sucks.

Why do we instantly blame ourselves versus realizing to ghost someone means that person is immature and, frankly, not deserving of us? This realization happened when I talked to friends or heard other women talking about being ghosted—making me instantly feel less at fault.

I created *Miss-Adventures Guide To Ultimate Empowerment For Women,* so we know we're not alone. Sharing our stories helps. Feeling less alone in our traumas, experiences, illnesses, etc., gives us mental, emotional, and spiritual strength to thrive in every area of our life. Ladies, sharing what we've gone through is our superhero power; half the time, we don't even realize the impact our stories will have in changing another woman's life. As a team of superhero women, we're always stronger when we bond, open up and stand together versus tearing each other apart.

Knowing a friend(s) or someone I've met had gone through something similar impacted my life tremendously—from when I was a child and throughout my adult life.

Losing my dad at the age of 20 had an extreme impact on my life. I labeled myself a loner in the *dead dads club.* As morbid as my club sounds, it fit how I felt. You can not understand the anguish, anger, disbelief, and desertion you feel until you lose a parent. Father's Day, his birthday, holidays, and, of course, the anniversary of his death were just cruel reminders that my dad was no longer alive.

Although I had siblings, losing my dad was different for me since I had my unique relationship and experience with him—like many siblings regarding their parents. In some families, death brings them closer or tears them apart—for my family, it wasn't one or the other.

Six years later, the Universe brought women who also lost their fathers at a young age into my life. These women knew and understood how I felt. Every muscle in my body engaged, my jaw clenched, the water built in the back of my eyes, and the inner disconnection—especially on *reminder days*—toward those who still had their dads grew. My inner turmoil felt less chaotic being able to talk about my dad and share my sadness and memories with these women who could relate.

The labels we give ourselves when we feel we're the only ones going through a trauma, struggle, experience, or illness are interesting. We tack on words to ourselves like guilt, shame, fear, disappointment, resentment, unworthy, blame, loneliness, etc.—until we realize we're not alone. Finally, someone gets it, has been there, genuinely understands. Thank you, God!

This, ladies is exactly why *Miss-Adventures Guide To Ultimate Empowerment For Women* was manifested.

All the stories in this book are a collaboration by women authors of different backgrounds, ages, nationalities, upbringings, careers, financial statuses, and experiences, who've opened their minds, bodies, souls, and hearts to connect, inspire, and show courage through their stories. These beautiful, touching, and sometimes heart-wrenching or humorous anecdotes are shared so we as women can find our inner strength and empowerment—leading our lives with love versus fear, faith versus doubt, and spiritual awareness versus chaos.

Miss-Adventures Guide to Ultimate Empowerment is not a solution book. There is no solution to dealing with heartache, trauma, death, illness, abandonment, body dysmorphia or any other emotion felt. However, there are practices we can use to help us not let these emotions become the driver's seat in our lives.

Harnessing your power and thriving in every area of your life means we control how we feel and whether or not we choose to be the victim. It also represents the power we decide to give away or not.

Finally, having a friend who was also adopted meant that finding my biological mother was a possibility. If my wish of finding another adoptee came true, then maybe, just maybe, my birth mother still wanted me.

Grab a cup of coffee, tea, or your favorite drink and immerse yourself in these incredible stories of love, strength, hope, inspiration, vulnerability, and intention, and let's empower each other one page at a time.

Xoxo,

Stephanie, aka; Miss-Adventures

CHAPTER 1

A JOURNEY TOWARD FINDING INNER LOVE

HOW TO RELEASE ABANDONMENT TRIGGERS

Stephanie Bailey, CYT, CMT

MY STORY

My stomach tightened and felt like it had dropped six inches—every muscle in my body stiffened, and my heart felt like it was beating out of my chest as I started reading.

"Hi Stephanie, are you Colleen Ennis's birth daughter? I found your information online?" *Is this a joke?*

It was early Spring 2007. I opened my brand new Facebook account and noticed I had a private message from a woman—I didn't know—named Stacey. I was only on Facebook for a few months after reluctantly being talked into signing up by my friend Nancy. I always thought My Space and Facebook were just a waste of time—why would anyone want random people to find them? Clearly, my disorientation reading this out-of-the-blue message was justified.

"Hi Stephanie, are you Colleen Ennis's birth daughter?" I stared blankly at these words.

I always believed I'd meet my biological mother. I didn't know how, when, or where; I just knew; however, four years ago, I let go of the silly, far-fetched notion I'd find Colleen. Honestly, I decided God either didn't intend for us to find each other or, as mournful as this sounds, she was dead. I had emotionally and mentally moved on—or so I thought. So why now?

"Hi Stephanie, are you Colleen Ennis's birth daughter?" I read again.

WTF, this can't be real? I immediately got off Facebook and called my friend Nancy.

As the phone kept ringing, my palms started sweating, and my entire body began to shake. *Pick up, pick up, pick up.* My heart continued to beat faster and faster. *Brring!* "Hi, Mama." Just hearing Nancy's voice, I felt my breath release from my lungs as if I had been underwater for several minutes.

Deep in my soul, since age seven, I had this unexplained feeling I'd one day meet my birth mom. So why couldn't I get my legs to stop quivering and my brain to connect to my words? "Stephanie, are you okay?" Nancy asked in a concerning voice. Then, as I started to form words, my mind yanked back in time. Trying to remember what past wish or hopeful experience I energetically sent Colleen that she finally received—in an exceptionally fashionably late way? As I started to remember, there were moments throughout my life that came flooding in.

Was this a spiritual SOS signal I sent in elementary school? I released a balloon in hopes of finding a pen pal (my birth mom) with my information attached—squealing like a baby pig, smiling ear-to-ear. I wrote my name, birthday, and address—very legibly for my age—on a card with a short note attached to a yellow balloon. Looking back, releasing balloons with children's information was a pedophile dream. However, I was releasing a balloon filled with faith and confidence—my special balloon would reach my birth mom. Shockingly, it did not.

As my mind returned to the conversation with Nancy, my legs continued to quiver, so I stood up and started pacing. "A woman I don't know just asked me if I'm Colleen Ennis's biological child." I couldn't stop walking back and forth as my body continued to tremble; I could feel my breath shortening to the point I thought I would pass out.

"Are you serious? Do you think it's her? Was there any way she could have found you?" Nancy asked with a calming but excited supportive tone.

My brain continued to wander backward in time again. Or was my intuition about meeting my birth mom enhanced the day my friend Karen told me in fourth grade she was adopted? I did wish and prayed to meet another adoptee. Besides my non-biological brother Charles, who was also in foster homes and adopted by the same family as me, the only other person I knew—who was adopted at that moment—was Karen.

Although my brother and I were close, knowing Karen was also adopted was different—my brother was three years older than me. He didn't like to talk about being adopted, plus Karen was a girl, too, who I connected with on a deeper emotional level.

Think, think! As I started racking my brain, trying to answer Nancy's question, I remembered that my doctor and I talked about being adopted and finding my birth mom about five or six years ago.

Dr. Redd was my OB/GYN, who became more than a doctor in my life. She genuinely cared about my health and me—which nowadays is rare. We had numerous talks about my adoption, amongst other things, and not knowing anything regarding my medical health, especially the possibility of any hereditary conditions. I remember sharing my birth mom's information and expressing how I have always wanted to find her, but I had no luck.

I tried contacting the hospital I was born at, hiring a private eye, meditating, praying, and even releasing a balloon. Dr. Redd offered to help. She placed the information I had on several websites for finding one's birth parent. But so many years had passed. I had given up and, frankly, forgotten. Four years before 2007, I decided I didn't need to find my birth mom to feel wanted, valued, or loved—the natural love and connection birth moms usually have with their biological children.

Don't get me wrong, my parents loved and raised me the best they could. I wasn't seeking out my birth mom to replace my parents. God gives us the parents who are meant to raise us; however, being adopted at two-and-a-half and growing up seeing how my two siblings resembled my mom and dad would trigger abandonment issues inside me.

Abandonment issues stirred inside my soul for as long as I can recall. I was in several foster/adoption homes—removed due to molestation in a few, and although I don't remember, deep in my soul and subconscious, the memories are there.

I grew up the youngest of four siblings. With all my issues, I was like the Tasmanian Devil wreaking havoc amongst my siblings and parents. Ahhh, a new two-and-a-half-year-old baby from hell spitting, twirling, hitting, and throwing things whenever I could. Hmm. What did anyone expect? From the day I was conceived from a rape, my soul only knew one thing—fight—like Brad Pitt in *Fight Club,* except even more aggressively—because my soul wasn't going to let anyone hurt me again. Unfortunately, I wish I could say that statement ended up being true.

Receiving this Facebook message about my birth mom kicked in feelings of fear of being left again. I immediately got off the phone with Nancy and called Dr. Redd.

Brrring, brring, brring! Pick up, pick up, pick up. Why did this feel like a horrible deja vu? All the yoga, breathing, and meditation exercises went out the door. *Brrring, brring, brr. . .* "Hello."

Hearing Dr. Redd's voice was like music to my ears. "Hi, Dr. Redd." My throat began to tighten. "This is Stephanie." I started rambling about the message. My breath was inhaling and exhaling out of my body so fast that I didn't know which one was doing what. "Slow down. Take a deep breath." Dr. Redd did her best trying to calm me. "Yes, I just received an email asking if you were still interested in meeting Colleen? She is searching for you."

Why did my heart burst with so much hope the day my wish came true when Karen told me she was adopted, but now it was filled with doubt, fear, and anger when my desire to find my biological mother came to fruition? Why was I letting my abandonment issues take over versus jumping up and down like a wildly excited kangaroo?

Inner love was something I searched for, like a desperate Charlie from Willy Wonka and The Chocolate Factory looking for the golden ticket. I believed everyone but me held the key to my happiness and self-worth. If others loved me, then I must be worthy of being loved. Right? If my birth mom loved me, why did she give me up? All the answers I excitedly wanted to know, I now feared, were just a Facebook message or phone call away—and I wasn't ready.

Worrying about being rejected is real. I spent so many years working on myself, being able to finally stand strong in the beautiful soul God created—me. So why was I being tested?

Life is interesting or a cruel joke. When we're handed—at times forcefully—shitty, challenging experiences, we tell ourselves we aren't worthy of being loved, having success, or, in my case, finding my birth mom. Colleen might have been the first person to leave me, but not the last.

I was 20 when my dad died of a sudden heart attack when he was away on a business trip. I barely had the keys to navigating life. Trusting people was difficult for me, and I completely trusted my dad. I was sad, angry, heartbroken, devastated, shocked, confused, and in disbelief—and my abandonment issues were swirling around me faster than the tornado in *The Wizard Of Oz*. I felt sick, alone, and abandoned by God.

Abandonment triggers were like the hounds of hell trying to dissolve my soul and take over my life: when my birth mom gave me up for adoption, all the homes I was placed in and out of, when my dad died, every wrong decision I made in my love life, friendships, and jobs. Now the hounds of hell were back, rearing their ugly heads, trying to take over my emotions by bringing Colleen into my life.

"I don't know if I'm ready to talk to her." My hesitation, surrounded by worries of rejection, started creeping in, and Dr. Redd felt this.

"If you aren't ready, as we discussed before, I will contact Colleen; this way, you know your medical information, and I can get a sense of her."

"Okay." As I sat down, my legs couldn't stop shaking, and I could feel sweat on my nose and above my lip. Now the wait began.

After Dr. Redd contacted Colleen and the multiple questions I sent to her friend Stacey—questions only Colleen would know the answers to—we confirmed Colleen was my birth mom. I called my mom—who raised me—and with her love and support, three weeks later, I called Colleen.

One of the biggest realizations I've had: God brings forth things in our lives when we're ready, not when we think we're ready.

Colleen came into my life once I worked on myself, finding my inner happiness and fully living my truth for years—becoming an empowered woman.

There were multiple pieces to my inner love puzzle—all the answers were always inside me, but I didn't know or believe it at the time. Convincing myself that I'd find one of these pieces to magically complete me through meeting my birth mom was the main reason we weren't united until I was 37. Not being united this late in age forced me to take a serious look inside myself and figure out the tumultuous crazy shit I was dealing with—internally and externally. I was on a self-destruction path, I wanted a new, loving direction, and I was finally open and ready.

One of my many steps to self-love was the day I decided to take my yoga practice more seriously.

I took several Bikram yoga classes back in 1996. But if you're not ready, it doesn't stick—like with most things in my life. It wasn't until I took a Vinyasa class at CorePower Yoga in 2002. I was introduced to CPY by my friend Angie; however, it was months later I took my practice to heart. And the beginning of the four-year mark when I decided to let go of finding my birth mom.

Yoga helped conquer a lot of my self-doubt, loathing, and fear. Stepping into a yoga class—this time by myself—and committing to practicing daily built my mental and, eventually, physical strength. My yoga practice wasn't just about the movements; it was much more profound. Being on my mat was a place I could ground and center myself, and learning how to breathe—the deep inhales and exhales—that I was lacking in life—cleared my mind, which guided my awareness of how awful I saw myself—igniting a desire to change.

As my yoga practice grew, so did my love for myself. I felt invincible; my inner love vibrated, and I was empowered and unstoppable. Once I mastered the art of forgiveness—starting with myself—my self-love reached an even higher plateau.

Working on myself, I could embrace who Colleen was, not the idea I created in my mind when I was younger. Letting go of expectation and the outcome, my conversations with her felt organic. Finally, meeting and hugging Colleen for the first time was better than a Hallmark card. Seeing her reinforced even more; she was my birth mom—like looking into a familiar mirror filled with pure joy. Little did I know how soon Colleen would be taken from my life.

"Hello." Trying to connect my words to my brain while looking at a blurry clock, searching for my glasses.

"Stephanie, this is Valerie" I could hear the trembling in her voice. "I've been trying to reach you. Colleen just passed away. I'm so sorry; I tried several times to reach you so you could say goodbye to her."

My mind tried to grasp the words Valerie just spoke—which weren't fully penetrating my foggy brain. My heart stopped. It felt like my soul was trying to leave my body—like a scene from *The Matrix*.

"What? I just spoke to Colleen a few days before Thanksgiving—she sounded exactly like herself." *Is this real? Is this happening again?* All my abandonment issues flooded around me like a title wave trying to pull me under an ocean. My breath shortened, and the water behind my eyes ran down my face. Gasping for air as I tried to capture my breath, flashes of Colleen fluttered in my brain.

On December 5, 2021, the hellhounds of abandonment came swirling back, trying to take over my life again, but this time, I had control. I was in the driver's seat.

Here's the thing, feelings of being abandoned can come when we least expect it. One week after Colleen died, I had a hysterical breakdown in a cupcake shop—picking up cupcakes made wrong—hours before my book release party. Luckily, this time I was in the driver's seat of my emotions. I knew my hysteria wasn't about the cupcakes—as irritating as it was that they were made wrong—and I knew what to do.

I put one hand on my heart and throat area and my other hand on my belly and took three deep breaths. I kept telling myself over and over again *I was okay. I'm okay. No One Has Left Me. No One is Leaving Me. God is Protecting Me.* I repeated this mantra until my heart and soul felt and believed this—which calmed the abandonment hellhounds from my life.

Feelings of abandonment (or any emotion) can come up anytime—it's okay. Pushing our feelings down or acting like they don't exist we internally create an emotional self-made prison. Yikes!

When I became a massage therapist and yoga teacher, I learned about chakras—our energy wheel points in the body. Chakras connect our mind, body, and emotions for energetic, emotional, and physical healing. Connecting chakra points in the body has not only helped my life in multiple aspects but have also been an effective tool for my love clients and massage clients.

I look forward to guiding you on this practice.

THE PRACTICE

First, a brief description of each chakra. We have seven total in our bodies, starting from your cervix/base of the spine to the top of your head.

1. The Root (red): Located on your cervix/base of the spine, represents home/family/basic trust—security/survival.

2. The Sacral (orange): Located in your lower abdominal area (between cervix and belly button), represents sexuality/creativity.

3. The Solar Plexus (yellow): Located on the belly button represents wisdom/power/ego/control.

4. The Heart (green): Located in the center of your chest represents love/healing/compassion.

5. The Throat (blue): Located on your throat area represents communication/speaking your truth.

6. The Third Eye (indigo): Located between your eyes represents intuition/insight/awareness/guidance.

7. The Crown (violet): Located on top of the head (and beyond) represents cosmic consciousness/spiritual connection.

Here's what to do when abandonment issues arise:

Place one hand, open palm—palm on chest, fanned fingers at an angle upward—covering your heart/throat chakras (think mid to high chest). Place the other hand—palm on the belly button, fingers fanned at an angle downward on the stomach, covering your root, sacral and solar plexus.

By positioning your hands like this, you are covering your major Chakra energy fields to help ground and calm you. This technique has helped me in recognizing and harnessing abandonment feelings when they arise.

Close your eyes or gentle look down and say this mantra (repeat this out loud):

I'm okay. I'm okay. No one has left me. No one is leaving me. God (Universe) is protecting me.

Say this mantra over and over again until you feel and believe this is true. Crying and screaming are welcomed—great for healing.

Once your body calms down and you feel grounded and centered again, touch your third eye chakra (space between your eyes) and say: *Thank you, Thank you, Thank you.*

Giving thanks recognizes your emotion and removes any power you were giving your abandonment (or any feelings) from taking over your life.

Light and Love,

Stephanie

Stephanie Bailey is the CEO of Miss-Adventures, LLC, has been a love coach/expert for over 26-plus years—she specializes in self-love, relationships, dating, break-ups, and being successfully happily single. Stephanie is also a #1 best-selling published author (best seller in six categories on Amazon), published writer, podcaster, CPY yoga teacher for over 13 years, and massage therapist for 22 years. Stephanie strongly believes in the power of prayer and affirmations to ignite and created the love, health, wealth, success, family, abundance, relationships, and prosperity we want in our lives. Stephanie's mission is to help empower women on their journey and create a clearer path for guiding them to self-love. Stephanie offers in-person and virtual love coaching sessions.

Stephanie is releasing a fun book about dating and men that's coming out soon. She also has a podcast with her sister, Tanya Garner, titled: *Sisters On Love, Life, and Keeping It Real.*

To stay in touch with Stephanie you can follow her on her social media platforms and visit her website: Miss-Adventures.com for Love Coaching advise, sessions, and packages.

"Self-love is always inside us, not something to seek out."

~ Stephanie Bailey

Connect with Stephanie:

Website: https://www.miss-adventures.com

Email: missadventuresseries@yahoo.com

Instagram: @miss_adventures_coach

Facebook Page: @missadventuresseries

Facebook Profile: stephanie.bailey.737

LinkedIn: linkedin.com/in/miss-adventures

Hubpages: miss-adventures.hubpages.com (relationship/love articles)

Clubhouse @stephanie266

YouTube: Sisters On Love, Life and Keeping It Real

CHAPTER 2

UNREQUITED

A RADICAL SELF-LOVE STORY

Tiffany McBride, MA, LCPC, RMT, ORDM

MY STORY

"Welp, that didn't work out."

"Again?" said my friend Mary.

"At this point, I'm starting to wonder if it's me or if I'm destined to be single for the rest of my life," I said, feeling hopeless.

"You just haven't met the right person yet," Mary said as she tried to ease my defeat. She sighed, "You really haven't been in a healthy, happy relationship before. I just think you don't know what it's like. It will happen."

I remember when I was six years old, my parents announced they were getting a divorce. I sat across from them, feeling bewildered. A frog crawled up my throat and tried to come out of my eyes, but I held back and swallowed my enormous wave of emotions. My parents seemed perplexed by my non-reaction, but I didn't know how to express my feelings at such a young age, so I sat there quiet and awkward. Instead, I exploited those suppressed emotions in the first grade by expressing anger, slapping my peers, talking back at teachers, and going to the principles office.

My father wasn't around very much. He'd be gone for months at a time out to sea on submarines. When he was around, I remember feeling small and fragile compared to his six-foot-six-inch demeanor. He scared me when he would get angry and snap at me, especially when he drank.

My mother kept my brother and me for the most part. She worked and did her best to raise two small children independently. I remember her being distant and in her own world, feeling alone and emotionally disconnected from her.

When I came home from school, I remember playing alone in the yard or escaping into the woods to play with frogs and snakes and make potions out of earthy material. I also escaped reality by watching television cartoons, which helped me process my emotions when I didn't know how to.

As a little girl, I fantasized about connection and relationships and acted this out when I played with my dolls. Many times I would play a couple having intimacy, and other times I would pretend to be a mom to a baby. It helped me feel connected since I couldn't find that connection with my parents. I felt alone, in another world, and abandoned by the prolonged periods without touch, emotional attunement, or reassurance.

Fantasizing for someone to rescue me from my emotional emptiness and sadness helped me through those highly distressing times at home. Daydreaming about being loved, swept off my feet, and carried away by a lover became a safe outlet where I could feel in control when my reality outside of me was not. Fantasy was where I could be unconditionally seen as lovable, worthy, and seen.

"I blame it all on my childhood and Disney Princess training," I said.

"Disney Princess training?" My friend Mary asked with a chuckle.

"Yea, all the programming I was fed as a little girl about how to be a princess and perfect and that the goal is to get the prince no matter the cost. Ariel, the mermaid, was my favorite character of all time. Do you know how much I love red hair? Ha. Yeah, that comes from a deep-seated program. She gave up her voice to be a human so she could get the boy. And it had to be done in three days. Or she lost her soul!"

"You are losing me," Mary said with a perplexed look.

"I was captivated with *The Little Mermaid* right after my parents' divorce. I wanted to be like Ariel. In the film, she gives up her most prized possession: her voice, her truth, her authentic self. She changes who she is to impress the prince. I learned that having a pretty face and a nice figure gets the boy. I absorbed the idea that rushing into a relationship within days, without authentic dialogue and only pure infatuation, was ideal. Otherwise, I would lose my soul forever!" I said dramatically. "This is where I began chasing and fantasizing for Prince Charming to come to save me and fulfill all my unmet childhood needs."

I continued, "As a kid, I was a tomboy and liked playing with the neighborhood boys. I would chase them around the playground and beat them up for fun." I laughed mischievously.

"I was assertive, bossy, loud, and awkward. By junior high, my peers bullied and humiliated me because I was different. At home, I also faced the same treatment by my evil stepfather and hushed-up mother. By 13 years old, I felt really alone, had no friends, and was in a dark place. So, to escape the depression and my suicidal thoughts, I would hide in my room and fantasize that a celebrity from one of my wall posters would come and rescue me."

"None of the boys I liked, liked me. Instead, they would spread rumors and tell lies. I joined the youth group in hopes that I'd find a boyfriend. I tried to become like everyone else to fit in. I felt ashamed of who I was and tried to get approval from everyone. I played a chameleon and had many social groups I belonged to, but no one really knew me authentically."

I paced the room, and my speech escalated. "When I started dating, I fantasized that my crush would fall madly in love with me, and we'd run off and get married. Instead, I picked partners who were not willing or capable of meeting those wishes. I've gone through every relationship feeling unfulfilled by their lack of emotional availability and inability to meet my unmet needs."

I paused, took a deep breath, and explained more, "At 19, I forced myself to like my first husband because I wanted to be rescued so badly. Instead, we became abusive to one another, leaving behind a tornado of childhood baggage. After that divorce, I hopped into bed with a few men and ran into another marriage. I annulled that after I found out he was using me for a green card. And again, I rushed into another relationship."

I shook my head, "Now, in my thirties, I've dated several people, dated several men who only wanted to be sexual with me but didn't want to commit. For two years, I chased that drummer guy. Remember that? He led me on with empty promises and eventually broke my heart when I found out other women were involved. And recently, I've tried dating younger men who are nicer but personally and emotionally immature. I've even dated women. Ugh!"

"I just think you haven't met the right person yet," Mary said again.

I looked at Mary, rolled my eyes, and made a gag motion by raising my finger to my mouth. "I've heard that for seven years now. We're going on eight years and over a hundred people I have met and dated. It's me, Mary."

I sighed, and with a quiet tone, I expressed, "Each year, it gets harder and harder for me to remain single. I am jealous of anyone who has a partner or is moving on with their lives and getting married. It's hard being the third wheel at family functions and outings. Holidays are the worst, and I want to hide from the world due to my shame of loneliness. I feel like a giant loser, despite how successful I am. I feel so bitter and numb about dating another person."

What kept me staying in this unrequited cycle?

Each relationship ended up the same. The rejection and abandonment I continued to face were draining and causing me health issues. It brought up painful feelings from my childhood when my parents rejected me or couldn't meet my needs.

In relationships, I've struggled to admit my wants or needs. Most times, if I did speak up for my needs, I'd have to face how unwilling and unable my partner was to meet them. Bringing up my needs always led me to feel disappointed and invisible. Therefore, it was always best to self-abandon and deny my needs in the first place. If I left my authentic self to be who other people were comfortable with me being, they'd give me approval, and I would feel secure. But it was a lie. I never felt safe because my acceptance was conditional, based on my willingness to self-abandon. Self-abandonment is when I reject, suppress, and ignore my needs, wants, and boundaries for others.

I bent over backward for partners who treated me like shit. I would smooth things over, make excuses, have clear conversations that went nowhere, teach them a better way, and give them too many chances. All of the emotional labor I was doing to make things work wasn't being kind. I was only enabling, self-abandoning, and even cooperating in the poor treatment I was receiving.

I may have been raised to believe that putting up with shit behavior was the cost to pay for a connection. I realize, though, that this is untrue. Letting things slide to keep the peace isn't nice; it's self-abandoning and only serves people who benefit from my being quiet. Even though I thought I was helping people out, being a team player, bridging gaps in a kind and generous way, and making my life and relationships work, I was over-functioning. Instead, I was enabling others to under-function and use me, blocking my ability to feel met, perpetrating imbalanced relationships, creating an unsustainable life, denying my actual needs, and draining my energy and time.

"The truth is," I told Mary, "the unrequited love is towards myself. I change and deny my needs. I become emotionally unavailable to myself by choosing these types of partners to be in my life. I abandon myself over and over in relationships. I give up my needs so I can fulfill others. I make myself invisible behind people who take credit for my work and don't value me as a respectable and worthy person. It is me."

A flame started to grow in my stomach and spread throughout my body. I didn't understand why I was feeling so angry. I just wanted to burn everything down—say "fuck it" to everything. This anger was a sign a boundary was violated; in other words, I was tired of the bullshit.

I knew if I stuck to my boundaries and needs, I'd be able to save my energy and time by focusing on myself. I could accomplish the goals I wanted to and embrace freedom by traveling around the world. Even though it was still lonely, and I didn't want to be single, I began to embrace it.

I decided to make commitments to myself and found people who could meet me in the emotional spaces I needed. I started to enjoy my life and adjusted it to bring me joy instead of stress. I stopped focusing on the lack and self-pity and put my heart into my hobbies. I started showing up for myself and working on the relationship with my soul. I learned to stop abandoning myself and speak up for my boundaries. Even though it was hard speaking my truth, and I have lost friends along the way, my life has become more manageable, peaceful, and steady.

When I date, I can identify the red flags and be grounded in the present moment instead of fantasizing about what could be. By the first date or conversation, I can determine whether or not my date will last. So far, I've been able to decline dates and feel confident in my decisions. Even though I'm still single at 39, I've learned to enjoy my life, whether or not I have a partner.

Below are the commitments and self-love statements I chose to make for myself.

MY COMMITMENT

I will no longer:

- Prioritize people who consider me an afterthought.
- Try to convince people to love or value me.
- Force relationships that have faded or no longer work for me.
- Tolerate one-sided relationships that haven't changed.
- Over-explain myself when the answer is no.
- Ignore my boundaries to make others like me.
- Alter my needs, goals, and values to be who I think they want me to be.
- Surround myself with unmotivated people or people who can't keep their word.
- Allow emotionally unavailable people into my life.
- Be silent or unclear about my wants and needs.
- Second guess my worth and the value I bring to the table.
- Be mean to myself when I mess up.
- Compare my work and life to others.
- Make excuses for unhealthy behavior (mine or others).
- Rush or feel pressured into things I haven't thought through or don't want to do.
- Rush myself to get over things.
- Tolerate chronically unfulfilling relationships.

- Abandon myself to give people what they want when it's not what I want.
- Go along with things that are not right for me just because I'm afraid people will leave.
- Accept unstable or poor treatment because I fear being alone if I speak up.
- Believe it's more important to have the other person than to honor myself.

I will:

- Start putting my needs first.
- Learn to keep boundaries.
- Learn to speak up for myself.
- Go to therapy and get vulnerable.
- Forgive myself for my past (I didn't know what I didn't know).
- Seek out a community to learn how to relate to others.
- Figure out what I love to do and do it.
- Find people who will listen and hold space for my vulnerable times.
- Journal more to figure out my thoughts and patterns.
- Practice mindfulness and meditation.
- Be responsible for my own feelings, wants, and emotions.
- Join a recovery program.
- Seek attachment trauma healing.
- Acknowledge and validate when I engage in fantasy for coping.
- Practicing self-compassion rather than shaming myself for fantasy thoughts.
- Communicate rather than withdraw when I'm disappointed.
- Seek out new coping mechanisms instead of fantasy.
- Surround myself with safe and vulnerable people.
- Be around people who accept me as I am (shit and all).

- Surround myself with people who make me feel seen, heard, and loved.
- Learn to love and reparent my inner child (inner child healing).
- Do things that only bring me joy and peace.

RADICAL SELF LOVE STATEMENTS

- Embracing my confidence and innate power is the key to my liberation.
- I dare to make my life up in any way I desire.
- I am an instigator for change for others.
- It's okay to be eccentric, rebellious, and unconventional.
- I love that I'm unpredictable and hard to contain.
- I must go to the extreme limits to find what inspires me.
- My most significant potential lies in prioritizing my experience and only doing what makes me feel alive.
- I love having exciting experiences and living a unique, provocative life.
- I don't have to second guess myself or compare myself to others.
- I am meant to discover radical self-love and acceptance.
- My capacity to love myself unconditionally and embrace an optimistic, joyous expression of myself is a gift to myself and eventually an inspiration to others.
- I will no longer cling to the status quo and be my unique self and trust that it's okay to be different.
- I want to live uninhibited and vibrantly.
- I will believe in myself and follow my own creative vision.
- I will remember that loving myself unconditionally is not a selfish act but my right and life's intention.

I hope this will help you love yourself more even though you may struggle with being single or can't seem to find the right person. Dating is hard enough; not loving yourself is even more complicated. I hope this will guide you to start putting yourself first and protecting your heart and soul instead of giving it away so easily. The more you respect and love yourself, the more you'll begin to attract people who can appreciate and love you too. Don't settle; you're meant to be loved fiercely.

THE PRACTICE

A WRITING PRACTICE

Tools needed:
- Paper
- Writing utensil

Reflect on the story I mention of Ariel from The Little Mermaid.

- Can you relate to it or any other Disney movie that reflected the same theme (a prince coming to save me?)
- Can you relate to my story of unrequited love?
- Have you struggled with fantasy thinking in relationships?
- Can you relate to self-abandonment?
- How often have you changed for someone hoping they would like you?
- How many times have you abandoned your own needs to seek approval?
- How many relationships have you been in that were emotionally unavailable or unable to meet your needs?
- Do you know what your unmet needs are from childhood?
- How many relationships have you rushed in or chased due to the fear of rejection or feelings of unworthiness?
- How many relationships failed despite you changing who you are?

Write any thoughts you have down.

Be aware of the ways we replace childhood family dynamics in relationships:

- Parents gave us conditional affection; therefore, we focus on trying to change unavailable people.
- Love has to be earned in the family; therefore, we try to be perfect and pleasing to be loved.
- Parents were emotionally unavailable; therefore, we get into relationships with emotionally unavailable people.
- Parents' behavior was erratic and unpredictable; therefore, we feel anxious about relationships falling apart.
- Family shunned emotional reactions; therefore, we feel uncomfortable with vulnerability.
- Parents instigated competitiveness between siblings or friends; therefore, we find ourselves in power struggles with our partners.

Can you relate to any of these? Write any thoughts down.

- Do you have a story of unrequited love?
- Do you know what your needs and wants are?
- Do you have a list of commitments you would like to create for yourself to keep your boundaries?
- What would your radical self-love statements be?
- What are some ways you can begin to start loving yourself fiercely and unconditionally?

Write any thoughts you have down.

For more stories and dating life lessons, please visit www.themaddelynnhatter.com

Tiffany McBride (She, Her, They, Them) is an LCPC, Reiki Master teacher, birth doula, expressive artist, and author. They run their private practice named Holistic Vibrations, LLC. They use holistic remedies and altered states of consciousness for those who struggle with trauma, addictions, women's issues, lgbtqai+ support, and those seeking a deeper spiritual connection. Tiffany is currently working on their doctorate in shamanic psycho-spiritual studies and is training to be a yoga teacher and a clinical hypnotherapist.

Their holistic and altered states of consciousness modalities include emotional release therapies (utilizing energy/positive psychology such as EMDR, EFT, MBSR, etc.), expressive arts therapies, energy healing with a foundation in Reiki, womb healing/doula services, sexual health education and empowerment, attachment trauma recovery, internal family systems, codependency recovery, motivational interviewing, transitional life coaching, spirituality, shamanic breathwork, hypnosis, somatic psychotherapy, and psychoeducation.

Tiffany hopes to eventually grow a community healing arts studio to help more people learn to express themselves and heal from their traumas and addictions. In Tiffany's downtime, they love to write, blog, paint, draw, play the ukulele and guitar, sing, be in nature, kayak, take photographs, read, go to concerts, hang with friends, and be a scholar.

Connect with Tiffany:

Website: https://www.tiffany-mcbride.org/

Facebook Group for Women/Non-Binary: SHEE: ReWilding The Sacred Yoni @ https://www.facebook.com/groups/1057289361484274

Instagram: https://www.instagram.com/witchycrowwmn83/

Dating Blog: 100 Men, 7 Years @ www.themaddelynnhatter.com

CHAPTER 3

MANIC DEPRESSION

HOW MEDICATION GAVE ME MY LIFE BACK

Tara Rose Ritchie, CPI

MY STORY

I wanted to drive off a cliff. Medication gave me my life back when my mind was in an oceanic funnel of confusion. I was in the driver's seat but couldn't see where I was going or where I had been.

After receiving my first diagnosis of manic depression while in college in 2008, I was so angry at the psychiatrist for simply doing her job. I went to her, knowing something wasn't right. I went there knowing I had three one-night stands in the past five months after being faithful to my former boyfriend for four years. I went there knowing I had just spent $500 of my $800 paycheck on a hurried shopping spree at Linens 'N Things. And most importantly, I went there knowing that bipolar ran in my family.

My friends reminded me I couldn't remember conversations we had the week prior. Admitting I had bipolar meant I'd also be absorbing the judgments I had about other people with the diagnosis, including my former roommate and my coworker's husband. *How could you marry someone who isn't mentally stable?* I initially thought to myself.

I refused medication for two more years. I relied on my mother's judgment, who lived out of state, and my chiropractor at this time. They wholeheartedly believed there was a natural treatment for every condition and that this diagnosis was incorrect. Chiropractic care is a licensed health care profession that emphasizes the body's ability to heal itself.

I was correctly diagnosed with organarexia (fear of inorganic food). I went from 112 to 92 pounds that year. Once the doctors treated my manic depression, much of the anxiety around food dissolved. Intensive outpatient therapy for my eating disorder was a vital part of my journey. The director read the definition of manic depression from the DSM-4 (Diagnostic and Statistical Manual of Mental Disorders). "Does any of this resonate with you?" She asked compassionately with her small white dog on her lap. I nodded yes. I felt relieved and defeated at the same time. Knowing I wanted to use natural methods in my healing journey, they quoted research that showed exercise and supplements could help with mild to moderate depression; however, medication was necessary to treat chronic depression. My mother got on the first redeye flight and helped me to check into a psychiatric hospital the next day. None of this would have been necessary had I started medication two years earlier.

At 25 years old, I sat in the psychiatric ward, which was a small concrete box that felt like a jail cell. I was here for several hours before they transferred me to an actual hospital room with a bed and doting nurses. I stayed here for five days. I was so angry. I felt like a victim. I felt abandoned by my mother and aunt after they dropped me off. They let the hospital feed me, and my soul craved to be fed by my mother, so I did not eat. My mother taught me only to eat organic food, and I obliged, hoping she would stay close. I moved in with her, and we spent every day together for the next three months. We tried chakra clearings and vitamin powders marketed for bipolar.

Unfortunately, none of this was making a difference. I continued to swing up into hypomania for two weeks, followed by a deep, debilitating depression for two weeks. I felt clear and energized for a day or two between episodes, then my mind returned to being fuzzy, and my body felt heavy again.

After three months of this, my stepdad said, "You don't have a choice. You're going back to the hospital." I felt cornered as I leaned back over the black marble countertop to get away from him. And then I exploded, hurling my fist into his chest. He was stunned but didn't move. He was quiet, grabbed his jacket, and left through the garage with his head down. Once my mom returned home, she immediately came to my stepdad's defense again. *How could she be so blind? I just want to shake her.* I wanted her to stand up for me, her flesh and blood daughter. My mom became so numb she wasn't even aware she was living with a man that enjoyed intimidating women.

I remember when I was eight years old, my mother missed an exit-only sign on Highway 36, and the fight that erupted has haunted me ever since. My stepdad and mother couldn't stop yelling at each other, so they stopped the car on the side of the highway and got out. My stepdad pushed my mom, and she collapsed onto the pavement of I-25, cracking the back of her head open. Later that evening, I took big, slow dinosaur steps into the bathroom where my mom was trying to stop the gushing blood from her head, which was profusely dripping in the tub, making the water strawberry colored. I thought she was going to die. My stepdad just sat there. His ice-cold blue eyes followed my trembling steps. "Good night, Mom." I thought my good night would be a forever goodbye. I couldn't imagine a day without my mother.

I believe the combination of this childhood trauma and my genetic predisposition triggered my manic depression into full expression when I was 24 years old.

"You really scared him," my mom said after my stepdad left the house. *Finally,* I thought. After she went to bed, I gave the small Benadryl dose I took every night to Lancelot, their beloved greyhound, to help him sleep more soundly. I needed to make my escape, so I stayed up all night as if I had just had an epiphany—I had.

I'd never see that man again. And when I slid out the back sliding glass door, there was no sound. No barking. No alarm. There was simply a moonlit sky illuminating my journey home. I wanted to run down the hill with my duffle bag, but my feet crept, step by step. I tried to start my gold Ford Taurus I inherited from my bompa (grandpa). He recently passed, and I knew he guided me on this journey. I slid into the tan cushioned seat, as I had for the past four years while at college, but it didn't start this time.

"Come on. Please! Not now," I whispered and rested my head on the steering wheel. Even though it had just hit 100,000 miles, there was only one reason it wouldn't start. I perked up when I realized what it was. I popped open the hood, slid the hook underneath the latch, and propped it open. My battery wires were unattached. *That's a simple fix,* I thought as I slipped back into the driver's seat. My stepdad already knew my next move. It was not the first time I had tried to get away from him. However, this time I escaped and took a three-day road trip before I nestled into the Rocky Mountains of Boulder, Colorado.

Seeing the Colorado mountains reminded me of when my dad wrapped me in Mexican woven blankets and cradled me to sleep in Taos, New Mexico, where I grew up. My eyes filled with tears as I finally felt the security I craved.

I slept deeply beneath a dark sky before Amanda, my best friend, picked me up the following day. We sang Journey songs on our way to the Flatirons Mall—instead, she drove me to a medical facility and then stated sternly, "You have a choice. You can take medication now, or you will be on your own after this." Instantly my teeth wrapped around my clenched hands as I pondered the words coming out of my best friend's mouth. I collapsed in my seat as I thought about all the years we had together, and I just wanted us to go back to when life was fun. Big tears filled my eyes and dripped down onto my lap. This felt so serious. She was my last friend on Earth. I was frightened, but I trusted her.

Following her warily, we floated up the elevator. One, two, three beeps before the elevator doors opened. Dr. Lee was a tall man with soft brown eyes and glasses. As I released a deep breath, he extensively discussed how all my medical appointments for manic depression would go. Since there wasn't a blood test for my disorder, I had to rely on this single conversation and trust him.

Is this really medicine? People go to school for eight years for this. I processed one thing he said: "You'll still be able to be a mom, and you'll be more stable after you have a baby." He continued: "Because you don't have insurance, I'm going to prescribe lithium, which is a salt that only costs six dollars per bottle." Lithium ended up being an excellent substitute for the Benadryl I was taking. I no longer woke up listless. I slept a lot, sometimes 12 hours a day. I slept to prevent waking up to my hangover from over two years of erratic behavior and a childhood filled with crazy. The difference in this medical appointment was that I was not sitting in a room alone with a stranger. I was sitting next to my best friend, and I trusted her.

This doctor was a friend of her mother, Marilyn, who also worked in the medical system. Specifically, the Western medical system—the one I feared. I didn't fear needles, homeopathic pills, or herbs with unpronounceable names that tasted like dirt. My parents had utilized Eastern medical practices for years. I trusted these methods with every fiber of my being. My parents originally denied that I have the condition and still sometimes do.

In the next two months, I was fired from two waitressing jobs, each lasting precisely one month. Marilyn knew I couldn't give my all. "I love having your company while my husband travels for work," she said lovingly and invited me to move in with her. It was four years before I moved out. It took an entire year to find the right medication and become stable. In that first year, I desperately wanted to feel like a normal 27-year-old again, so I moved in with a roommate for a month and went back to what was familiar: having energy, going out dancing, and drinking with people my age. Without Marilyn, who knew my medical history and how meaningful it was to just get up every morning at 7 a.m. and have breakfast together, I quickly declined. Much to my detriment, I stopped taking Lithium. I simultaneously stopped sleeping and either laid in bed awake all night or found a strip club to enjoy sexual energy. I increased my flirting, and there was no one who didn't feel my presence. I wore bright pink sarongs and tight miniskirts that closely wrapped my body. I went home with one tan Brazilian man, then a sexy Italian, and a curvy peach that week. Later I just felt so disgusted with myself that I wanted to lay in bed all day. And I did, for the next two weeks. Painfully watching my rapid decline, at Marilyn's urgency, I started a new medication.

Lexapro worked well for a few months. Then I started Seroquel and started sleeping deeply for the first time in three years. A member at the gym I worked at walked up to me and said, "You look so much brighter. Did something amazing happen to you?" He wanted to know if I was in love or just got back from vacation, something to attribute this glowing face to. I was apprehensive about revealing that it was just good brain chemistry and the result of a new medication. I stopped taking Lexapro, and the magic happened when I added Lamictal. It was such a life-changer for me.

Most people with manic depression take two medications or more. The psychiatrist must be so careful with anti-depressants because as soon as they become effective, you have the potential to go back into mania. Conversely, with too strong a medication for mania, you can plunge into depression. Like flying an airplane with turbulence, the flight can get bumpier before you land. "Medications are an essential part of a treatment plan. They won't cure you, but they will help you keep your moods in balance so you can do the things you need and want to do"[1].

No one expects a child in an abusive home to grow up and be happy, healthy, and well-adjusted with effective coping mechanisms. Likewise, I didn't expect medication and a different home environment to have such a positive impact. I could have normal-looking routines like working, cleaning, and dancing to Justin Bieber with my nieces, even if I did not feel normal on the inside. Even if I wanted to erupt, I knew not to. My newfound stability, luxurious housing, and expensive cute dogs depended on being well-mannered. For this type of stability, I was dependent on medication. As diminished as my former identity felt, I was finally safe.

Although it can be painful to feel as if everything is standing still and you're locked inside, you're not dead. You're not locked in a prison. Instead, you're locked in a brain and physiology that cannot function without proper medical treatment.

It was important for me to realize that it's okay to shut down the misfiring operating system for months or years and let the dust settle. There are people to apologize to and amends to be made, but the minimum return I was able to give to my family and friends was to take medication. That was the highest form of love and respect for their patience and care. So many people will leave your life due to your erratic behavior, and it was very lonely for a while. I had to be okay with this because while they already knew how to take care of themselves emotionally, I was still learning, and it provided a great example of necessary boundaries.

The goal is not to recover the losses but to be grateful for your friends and the stability you now know. It takes a high degree of self-awareness, integrity, and honesty to say, "This is my mood disorder," versus "This is me being an asshole." However, now that I know the difference, it's my responsibility to do everything in my power to remain stable.

1) https://www.webmd.com/bipolar-disorder/guide/medications-bipolar-disorder

I'd prefer that no one read about the chapter of my life where I was at my worst: sleeping around, driving 90 mph on the highway, drinking, and yelling loudly at my friends and family. However, nearly everyone will encounter someone in their life with manic depression. Without treating this, life is hell.

With treatment, I have owned a Pilates studio, gotten married, had a baby, and now own a home. I take none of these precious parts of my life for granted. It was all possible because of the psychiatric treatment I received. I do have a holistic approach now with counseling and neuro-acupuncture.

Pregnancy and nursing were also challenging with mood swings due to hormonal changes. Fortunately, I could stay on my medication and adjust the dosage. Remembering not just how much I respect and love myself but how much my family loves me is what keeps me going on the days when I have no hope or goals for myself. Most days, I can lift myself up by the bootstraps, but my medication is really what makes my life functional and fabulous. And it's what has kept the relationships I have strong. I realize that I am the most crucial factor in my recovery and continued stability.

I never take my stability for granted. Each day I feel like I'm in a normal state is a huge blessing to me, my family, and the world. Ultimately, I can't do any good for anyone else if I'm not at my best. I'm incredibly grateful for all the support and knowledge I've obtained so that I can share this with you.

THE PRACTICE

1. Identify your triggers and avoid them. Instead, surround yourself with empathetic family and friends.

2. Live with an understanding roommate and a pet. It's super helpful to have someone be a mirror for you. At the very least, check in with someone every day.

3. Find the right medication from a psychiatrist you vibe with. This will probably take several tries.

4. Find a psychologist to help you manage the many life changes. Once I had the right medication, I completed six months of EMDR therapy. "Eye Movement Desensitization and Reprocessing is a psychotherapy treatment that was originally designed to alleviate the distress associated with traumatic memories (Shapiro, 1989a, 1989b)"[2].

5. Get on a set sleep, work, and exercise schedule. Get up every morning at the same time of the day, especially when depressed. When manic, sleep whenever you can. Ideally, once you have medication that helps you sleep, take it every night at the same time and wake up at the same time every morning. Get sun on your full body and eyes without contacts or glasses before 10 a.m. This will help with melatonin, serotonin, and Vitamin D hormone production.

6. Take a high-quality multivitamin with an a.m. and p.m. component with methylated folate, selenium, and zinc, as well as fish oil and omegas. All are shown to be helpful with manic depression.

7. Use a journal to write down how you feel daily on a scale from -5 to +5. An ideal mood range is -2 to 2, so make a note of your triggers on the days that mood swings increase.

8. Love yourself with all your flaws. Your life has a purpose. You may just not know what that is yet, so be patient with yourself like you are with a valued pet.

2) https://www.emdr.com/what-is-emdr/

Tara Ritchie lives in Denver, Colorado, and enjoys the Venezuelan cooking of her husband and the delight of their two-year-old while they salsa dance together. She is a Certified Pilates Instructor and Licensed Avatar ® Master. Since 2006 Tara has been delivering the Avatar® Course, which is a three-section self-empowerment training guided by a worldwide network of licensed Avatar Masters. It is a series of experiential exercises that enable you to rediscover yourself and align your consciousness with what you want to achieve. She used these belief management tools to integrate much of her childhood experiences and learn to live deliberately. It was especially helpful in 2017 when she built her dream Pilates studio before discovering her passion for real estate and design. She has a home renovation company with her husband, and after teaching for 20 years, she now makes Pilates workout videos for postpartum mommies. Growing up skiing in the Rocky Mountains, she developed a passion and knowledge for the fitness industry that continues to motivate her to instill a healthier and active lifestyle in everyone she meets. She offers virtual and in-person coaching. She believes Pilates is the best way to achieve grace in your body without having to endure the years of dance choreography classes and performances that she did. It has given her an edge in preventing injuries and gaining core strength. She brings exceptional skill and care to each of her clients. This is true whether she is helping someone design their home, body, or lifestyle.

Connect with Tara:

Instagram: https://www.Instagram.com/PilatesVitalDenver

Facebook: https://www.Facebook.com/PilatesVitalDenver

YouTube: Pilates Vital by Tara Rose Ritchie

LinkedIn: https://www.linkedin.com/in/TaraRoseRitchie/

Twitter: https://www.Twitter.com/TaraRoseRitchie

Blog: https://PilatesVitale5280.wordpress.com

Website: https://www.PilatesVital.com or TheAvatarCourse.com

Shop with me: https://www.beautycounter.com/tararoseritchie

CHAPTER 4

POWERHOUSE

BUILDING A PURPOSE DRIVEN LEGACY

Anna Pereira

"Keep away from people who try to belittle your ambitions. Small people always do that, but the really great make you feel that you, too, can become great."

~ Mark Twain

MY STORY

Emerging from my basement to head out to the store caused a panic attack. The tightening of my chest. The super sensitivity to noise, light, and the air on my skin. The pressure pushed in on every square inch of my body.

Everyone is staring at me.

Get your stuff. Get back in the car. **Get home.** The words echoed in my mind.

My heart raced.

Breathe. Breathe. Breathe. Don't black out. Just get home.

Alas, I'm home safe. Alone. Safe. Alone. Back to work. . .

Flashback:

"Sure, I'll have a drink. Can you buy me a bottle?"

"Which champagne would you like?"

"Dom Pérignon. I'll be out after my set."

Before I decided to go all-in on myself and my dreams of having a T-shirt collection that empowered women, *Super Sexy,* was my brand because I believe it's a woman's confidence that makes her truly super sexy! I was up on stage shakin' my ass as a go-go dancer pullin' loot like nobody's business.

Why would I quit a job that brought me freedom, red carpets, cars, a house, vacations, and a dope wardrobe (yes, I said dope), to start my own venture into the unknown? Dreams, baby!

If you have a dream, no matter what is stacked against you, no matter the sacrifice, no matter the blood, sweat, and tears necessary to make it happen, you go for it.

It's a calling. A compelling drive that you must do whatever it is you need to do once you're inspired and the dream is sparked.

You come up with the funding. You teach yourself what you don't know. You put in the hours and hours. You show up!

I had it bad—the need for my creative self, combined with the desire to empower women, blinded me. My mission was to change the world with a T-shirt!

Okay, a T-shirt wasn't going to change the world, but the messages were— my mission would and did. Well, they changed at least a few lives.

Messages like "Flavor of Your Lifetime" with an ice cream cone design I custom-made per order. My client can choose the shirt style and color of airbrush paint (ice cream flavor)—Strawberry, chocolate chip mint, etc.

I created their custom order and bedazzled it with Swarovski crystals, all lovingly applied by hand one at a time, knowing the goddess wearing this was indeed the flavor of someone's lifetime. Knowing she was sharing that empowering statement emblazoned across her chest was amazing, and I felt doubly awesome because she had a hand in customizing her one-of-a-kind design!

"Anna. I just saw Adrianne Curry wearing your shirt on her show. I'll call the producers to get you some still shots for your media kit," my publicist informed me.

I had celebrity clientele. My shirts were on TV. Selling online. Showing up in Us Weekly magazine and other publications. In award show gift bags. Things were moving along in my small business.

It was time to leap again. I decided to take my custom-made-to-order brand to production.

This was so exciting! I had my samples printed at a local but huge facility that printed thousands of items a day for retailers and manufacturers we're all familiar with.

I started booking buyer's shows and finding showrooms in Los Angeles and on the east coast to represent my line.

Here we go, baby! On the way to the big time!

Until I wasn't.

If you're interested in knowing how difficult it is to be in the fashion world, I highly recommend watching *The Curse of Von Dutch: A Brand to Die For.*

Watching that docu-series brought me back to the struggle I endured. I could never explain the mental, emotional, and financial stress I went through. I cried during certain parts as I relived how hard it was and what I went through *alone* as a business owner in the fashion industry.

That was the beginning of the end of Super Sexy.

It's just as well. In the day-to-day, it was a constant struggle to remain hopeful and sure, and steady. I had no idea back then what mental health was or how to navigate and fortify myself—what spiritual resilience I needed. Or how important the emotional support of loved ones who were just there for me would be.

Anxiety was my way of life.

I had no anchor in my life. I was single and had no business partner either. I was completely and literally alone.

"You are an entrepreneur?" Both a statement and a question. Nancy was a well-known psychic medium who worked with law enforcement, with a two-year waiting list for a reading.

"Well, I am a designer."

"You are an entrepreneur."

"Okay. . ."

At that moment, I realized *yes*. I am an entrepreneur. I had never thought of myself as one.

en·tre·pre·neur
/ ˌäntrəprəˈnər, ˌäntrəprəˈno͝o(ə)r/
Noun
1. A person who organizes and operates a business or businesses, taking on greater than normal financial risks in order to do so.

Seeing myself with a new identity was a real shift in awareness. I felt into myself as a risk-taker—a dream believer. I felt justified and validated in a strange way.

I felt a lot less "What the fuck am I *doing?!*" with any need to explain myself. This shifted to respect for my dreams, inner knowings and being the magic and worth of who I was.

Maybe I felt people would have a clearer idea about the "who" I really am by identifying as an entrepreneur. A designer can be someone who just doodles all day, but an entrepreneur risks it all.

Those risks weighed heavily on me. It was difficult to have a romantic relationship. Financial hardships and borrowing against the house were realities. Eating PB&J to make ends meet was another.

I went from the red carpet, money showers, and champagne to dwelling in my office/art studio/basement day in and out.

The day came for me to give up on the dream and get a job.

The first interview out of the gate landed me the division head position in a 55-million-dollar company heading a 15-million-dollar division. Coming from a sole proprietorship to head a division that accounted for nearly 30% of their revenue was pretty huge.

But I came in and did a great job. I designed and developed a product line that sold out before it even hit the loading dock. This was the third product **in the company's 50-plus-year history** that had achieved this.

However, I didn't belong. I secretly hated that job. There was no soul reward. How was I contributing to my legacy? Dog clothing was not my road to get there.

Others took notice of the success I was building for that company. Being headhunted with the opportunity for a significant pay increase by a huge company in Manhattan was met with a grinding halt thanks to a non-compete which left me, in the end, jobless.

Things happen *for* you, not *to* you.

Back to T-shirts!

In the past, I created by airbrushing. This time, I learned screen printing to create my designs and mixed in hand-dying and hand painting to complete my unique wears.

I invested in supplies and started anew with a new direction on my designs, to uplift and empower through energy and spiritually-infused designs.

"Blessed. To know that you're blessed. . ." as I pointed to my shirt. It was my favorite design and one of my best-sellers. I was wearing "Blessed" in big gothic font with blue and purple splatter in my 2010 News 12 New Jersey interview with Alicia Vitarelli.

"Blessed" was my most popular design, along with my Guardian Angels. I really loved printing, designing, and custom-creating clothing. Even as I write this, I crave to be back in my studio, printing, dying, and paint-slinging!

If you'd like to watch that interview and get inspired by a girl and her T-shirt line, the video is posted here:

https://www.thewellnessuniverse.com/world-changers/annapereira/

Little did I know that was another brick in the foundation to build The Wellness Universe. Inspiration and moving the needle for those in search of a foundation, transformation, confidence, spirituality, and feel-good resources.

I share all of this because it takes fortitude, resilience, determination, curiosity, consistency, finances, hustle, grit, integrity, alignment, awareness, and most of all, solid relationships to be successful.

Where am I today?

Fast forward through the muck, mire, heartbreak, back-stabbing, bankruptcy, marrying my twin flame, and living a wonderful life between Portugal and New Jersey, to building the mecca for wellness—here I stand.

I couldn't have arrived at this place alone. Yes, my talent, vision, and spark started it all, but without my relationships and being grounded in who I am, the value I bring to the world, and showing up, I could never be a powerhouse.

Going from social media influencer (and between you and me, I think "influencer" stuff is kinda bullshit) with nearly one million followers to creating The Wellness Universe in 2014 was fun, but what really moves the needle? My relationships and the wellness projects and programs we create together to help people. The lives we transform. The way we make the world a better place, one person at a time.

Over in The Wellness Universe, we believe happy, healthy, healed humans lead to peace globally.

It's through showing up, being consistent, knowing and *believing* in the long game, and being honest with my community and myself that gifted me with the community I'm surrounded by. I've had opportunities to help more people and multiple investors and co-owners who took little more than a phone call to join me after years of being *me* and always leading with integrity.

As we move the needle in the world of wellness and well-being, I no longer stand-alone, and what has made me a powerhouse is my vision, commitment to myself and my values, consistency, trust, mission, and blessed relationships.

My legacy is purpose-driven and a growing, thriving business. If you're reading this, **believe in yourself,** and feed your mind, heart, and soul so you too can excel and become even more fulfilled, successful, and a powerhouse in your own right.

THE PRACTICE

As mentioned, being a powerhouse and purpose-driven has little to do with size, strength, credentials, experience, and such. It has everything to do with who you are, your reputation, how you show up, your ability to pivot, and the action you take.

You can learn systems, strategy, and other things along the way, but *who* you are and how you show up for yourself and others is where your core strength and trust lies.

Just like not all mothers are a mom. Not all who work hard or pursue a dream are a powerhouse.

A powerhouse moves the crowd. A powerhouse is committed. A powerhouse is reliable and dependable. A powerhouse affects positive change. A powerhouse inspires.

HOW TO BE A POWERHOUSE

- Know Yourself and Your Core
- Have a Mission
- Show Up
- Be Consistent
- Be Trusted
- Know the Road Ahead and Be Realistic
- Have Great Relationships

Being a powerhouse is not in what you're offering, selling, or doing at a specific moment; it is the totality of who you are, what you do, how you do it, and who you are surrounded by.

For what reason and why would people keep coming back to you or to me? Here are the practices that empower you (referencing the bullet list above) to own the powerhouse status you deserve:

1. **Know You. Be True to You.** What does this mean? Get in touch with yourself through faith, self-development, and establishing

core values, which lead to setting boundaries. We've all heard, "If you don't stand for something, you will fall for anything." This is essential to a strong, steady foundation—the confidence you need and the unwavering courage and strength you will have to summon when you're making decisions—tough decisions.

2. **Be a Compassionate Inspirational Leader.** Leadership development is essential. Be a better listener than a speaker. See people for who and all that they are. Ask your heart for guidance. Don't always listen to your brain. Love-based decisions are formed in your true heart—fear-based decisions in your head. Develop your intuition and tap into your God voice inside you.

3. **Have a Self-Care Routine.** What do you do for yourself consistently that feeds your mind, body, and soul? Do you meditate, pray, exercise, write, or create? Do you put time aside to do breathwork, take a class or commune with a group? Self-care is essential to build resilience, mental and emotional fortitude, and connection with self and the world around you. You will also discover that by healing hidden wounds and trauma with many self-care routines, the stronger you'll become emotionally, mentally, and physically. You will be a better leader.

4. **Keep Greatness Around You.** Once you have all of the other points addressed and nurture them, this is my biggest amplification to your personal joy and personal and professional success: **Build great relationships.**

Keep great people close. Nurture wonderful relationships. When you have alignment, and it feels good in your gut, be an amazing human.

Fluffy, transactional relationships never worked for me. I need to feel nourished in my relationships. I look to see someone as I desire to be seen. I want to be excited to speak with you! I want to get behind what excites you, even if I haven't a clue what it is!

I want to feel safe and know I can trust you to reach out to you for your love and support.

Integrity-based relationships—I show up as that, so I attract that.

I respect diverse opinions and see how that can make me grow. I allow people to be themselves, and I cheer on the great aspects of those in my life. If I feel contrary and voice it, I know I will at least be heard and respected.

Your personal relationships are the most important. If you're having issues in your family or marriage, those need to be addressed. Our emotional and important relationships will impact professional success, health, financial well-being, and so on. Those must be "right." You cannot run away from core, important relationships.

"You all may be aboard right now. This is new and exciting, and we all have what it takes to make The Wellness Universe a success. In fact, it will be a success, but it's your personal choices that will keep you in and successful or count you out."

I spoke those words to three women in my living room the day we all met in person to come together and create The Wellness Universe. Within 12 months, only I and my former co-founder Shari Alyse remained. Without getting into detail, because of personal issues/decisions, the others fell away.

Relationships are the foundation of lasting business success and a happy life. Our relationships are essential to feel love, give love, explore, grow, expand, share, amplify, impact, and be the contribution to the world we're here to be in.

We're not meant to be or live alone. We're not solitary creatures. Even plants need pollination through their relationship with bees, birds, and butterflies to produce seeds.

Your seeds—your ideas, intentions, creations, efforts, products, services, purpose (whatever you consider your seed)—I'm willing to bet, need a witness, an audience, a cheerleader, a mentor, a helper, a user, or a recipient for you to see your seed grow into something spectacular.

Who are you sharing or gifting your seeds to?

Evaluate your relationships. Keep those that are mutually beneficial and release the ones that deplete you.

Stay the course. You have a big dream. Inspired dreams are not given out without intention by the Universe. Believe that!

So, what are you going to do with that dream? Hmm, **Powerhouse?**

 **Anna Pereira** is Soul Ventures Corp CEO and President, The Wellness Universe, Head Goddess and Chairwoman, Wellness for All, CEO. As a WBENC-certified woman-owned business, her mission is to make the world a better place. She's an inspirational leader, mentor, and connector for business owners who are changing the world. As an author and creator of wellness events, projects, and programs, Anna is an expert at showcasing, promoting, and supporting the world's most talented wellness professionals.

Anna lives between Portugal and her birthplace, New Jersey, with her husband, sports expert and investor Hugo Varela. The couple has adopted pets, and an African Gray, Big Red.

Anna enjoys painting, writing, and being creative in her hobbies. She enjoys finding balance in nature or at the beach and being with friends. She's dedicated to serving her calling and leaving her legacy as a conduit for change by bringing more health, happiness, and well-being to the world through collaborations. Learn more about Anna and The Wellness Universe at https://www.thewellnessuniverse.com/world-changers/annapereira/

CHAPTER 5

ENDING THE CONTROL

GUIDE TO TAKING BACK YOUR LIFE

Cynthia Webster

MY STORY

As I sat in the backyard of my home, looking at the lake nearby, I suddenly felt awakened. *What the hell are you doing? You deserve to be treated so much better than this.*

I realized the life I was living had to change. I would no longer be treated with disrespect and loathing. I would no longer be controlled by him. I had to figure out a plan to get out.

It was a Saturday night. Most people were getting ready for a night out—maybe at the movies, dinner, or the local bar. Not me. I started to pack my belongings. I looked around the house I thought would be mine forever with the husband I thought was the one. It stirred memories of the wedding we had in the backyard. It also stirred memories of the many phone calls and conversations we shared. Some of them were good and full of love. Others were so hurtful my eyes would fill with tears. I didn't realize at the time that many of the hateful words were drug-induced. He began using various drugs, and I was the easy target of his altered state of mind.

I had to get out of the toxic environment and regain the confidence and strength I once had.

The next morning, I got a ride to a local motel and stayed for a couple of days. It was close to my job I needed to figure out a plan to get my life back. I threw my bags on the bed and called my family. "Mom, I just wanted to let you know I left. It's not getting any better. I'm kind of scared it might get worse. I'll call you soon to let you know what I'm gonna do." I didn't go into detail, though; I just wasn't ready.

I had one good thing from the beginning, a steady job. I knew I'd have a steady income, and I just had to find a place to call my own. I realized the motel I was staying in would have to change; however, because I had no car and needed to be able to use public transportation. I moved to another hotel and started to look at apartments. I'd have to get a second job to afford the deposit, as well as furniture and a car.

I had to stay focused on the plan, but: *I know this is the right thing for me, but I have no support. What if I get sick and can't work? What if I lose my job? What about the extra bills to pay? What if everyone thinks I'm a failure?* I had to maintain both jobs, save as much as possible for the deposit, and keep the doubt and fear at bay. I couldn't deal with it yet.

I worked on keeping the negative thoughts out of my head; I reminded myself that I overcame struggles once before by paying for college by myself. I reminded myself how I listened to my angels as they guided me through it all. *Thank you, ladies! I'm gonna need your help! We got this!*

The one good thing about not having a car was that I had to walk to some places. I got some exercise but was also able to clear my head and listen to music. This always helped me to feel energized and empowered. I learned my way around town on foot and found some quiet places to enjoy.

It only took a month to save enough money, and it felt so empowering to sign the lease for my apartment. I could now move the rest of my stuff to a permanent place and concentrate on building myself back into the strong, confident woman I was before this. I found a job near the apartment, so I still had the extra money coming in. I still worked the other job, so I was back to two jobs. I still needed to get a bed. I also wanted to be able to see my family for the holidays.

I slowly made new friends and went out after work. I wanted to have fun. It had been so long since I was able to do that. I had unknowingly, gradually given my husband control over everything in my life. We moved away from my friends and family, so there was no support system for me. I didn't know anyone where we moved to, so I naturally relied on him for almost everything. I had a job when we first moved; however, eventually, he wore me down with all the complaining about leaving him to work, so I gave in and quit.

We finally almost ran out of money for the bills, so I got a job. "What do you think you're doing, getting a job? You're supposed to stay here and take care of me and the house. I don't want you around anyone else."

I truly enjoyed the job, but again, the complaining started. I didn't pay attention this time. I was going to keep this one. I was starting to stand up for myself but had to be careful. I knew if I pushed too much too soon, the physical abuse would start.

A friend of his told him, "She's gonna leave you in six months."

He just laughed.

This was around the time I had the awakening in the backyard.

I didn't say anything to anyone about leaving, even my family. They were worried about me. "Are you sure everything is okay? You seem so quiet lately," Mom would say after talking on the phone.

I wasn't sure what he would do. I knew there was abuse in his family but honestly thought it wouldn't happen to us. I got nervous around him because, at one point, he locked me out of the house we were staying in. The only place I could go was the neighbor's house up the road. They let me in for a little bit. Eventually, he unlocked the door, laughing at me.

There was also an incident in which I went to the store because the phone wasn't working. They fixed it and I returned home. He tried it and said, "I thought they fixed this piece of shit!" The next thing I knew, a phone was flying very closely past my head.

Those two incidents reminded me that I had to be careful. I didn't have any extra money saved, and I didn't have anyone to help me. I called a friend, and she said, "I'm sorry. My husband doesn't want to get involved in this."

A small part of me felt defeated, but I knew this wasn't how a person should be treated by someone who is supposed to love them. Part of me wondered, *did he ever love me?* He was so controlling. If I was a few minutes late getting home, that automatically meant something was going on in his mind. I also endured many hateful phone calls when he was out of town working. He repeatedly told me, "I hope when I get home this time, you're gone. I can't believe how stupid and lazy you are."

After many of these phone calls and being told hateful things to my face, I started to believe them. I doubted my worth. I didn't realize until later that that was part of his plan. He wanted a shell of a woman who would do whatever he wanted.

As I started to reclaim my life, I realized there were many things I chose to ignore because I thought we loved each other. I thought if I was a better wife and didn't make any mistakes, it would get better. I thought if he stopped with the drugs, it would get better. I thought if he wasn't around certain people, it would get better. None of that mattered. He just wanted someone to control and treat him like the king of the castle. It didn't matter how I was treated.

I found out later, as the divorce was coming up, that he already found a replacement and that he was cheating on me the entire time we were together. I had suspicions about the cheating before I left but didn't investigate. It didn't matter anymore. I was leaving, so I didn't care.

As I look back on this part of my life, there's one thing I'd have done differently. I would have searched for a support group or counseling. I survived this on my own and did what I had to so that there was a roof over my head, food to eat, and a place to lay my head. All the determination helped me to achieve that, but part of me was still damaged. It took many years to realize that and to work on fixing it. I found many people who enabled me to see and let go of the hurt. Most importantly, I regained my strength and confidence.

THE PRACTICE

Whenever I feel down, I crank my playlist, which includes: "Fight Song" by Rachel Platten, "Fighter" by Christina Aguilera, "Stronger" by Kelly Clarkson, and "Survivor" by Destiny's Child, to name a few. I make a list of things I'm grateful for and say a prayer of thanks for letting me have another day.

Although the present-day offers many resources for people experiencing any type of abuse, I had very few options when I was experiencing it. Many places were still calling it a marital issue and not taking any action to protect or help the victim.

I relied on myself and my determination to succeed. I also leaned on my faith and the knowledge that my guardian angels were looking out for me. I took walks through the neighborhood and listened to music; this would calm and empower me. As I gradually achieved my goals, getting my apartment, buying a bed, and eventually buying a car, I regained my self-esteem and confidence.

My suggestion and advice for anyone looking for support and help:

1. When you're ready to leave, make sure to have a bag with a change of clothes, cash, cards, and photo ID. Any or all of these will make it easier for you.

2. Have a place to go: A women's shelter, trusted family members or friends, or a cheap hotel if necessary.

3. Find counseling and support groups to help build yourself back up.

4. Be sure to have your own means of financial support.

5. Set goals to take back your life: Your own apartment or house, your own vehicle.

6. Be proud of yourself as you make progress along the way. Never doubt your ability to overcome and move on.

7. This is the most important, do not feel like you are on your own. Many women have been through this. It's just a matter of seeking out the available resources. The mode of communication doesn't matter—internet, music, therapist, exercise, meditation. You need

to release the negative feelings (like not being worthy) and build up the confidence that you deserve all the beautiful people and things the world has to offer.

As I mentioned, this happened pre-internet. Some of the resources I used can be done anywhere. The most helpful to me was to write. I made a gratitude journal. I listed everything I was grateful for, such as waking up to live another day, family and friends, a place to lay my head, and a job to enable me to eat and get any necessities I needed. I wrote down my strengths and goals for the future. These are things that wouldn't have to be done daily but should be done at least weekly.

As the internet came into being, I was also able to find resources to support my healing and outlook. I honestly don't remember how I came across some of these people, but they have been most helpful to this day.

Resources:

- www.daniellelaporte.com She focuses on heart-centered feelings, and her truth bombs are always on point. Such as "Your soul is rooting for you."
- www.terricole.com She is a trained psychologist and author. Her latest book Boundary Boss was much needed as I realized that this was something I still needed to work on.
- www.tut.com Mike Dooley has many programs that he offers, as well as an email campaign called "Notes from the Universe." They can be very insightful and usually arrive with a message you need. His biggest tagline is "Thoughts become things."

The above resources are ones I still use today. I, too, have days where I need help and direction. Even years later, not every day is sunshine and rainbows. I keep going and pray that you will too.

- You can also reach out to the abuse hotline. Go to www.thehotline. org or text START to 88788, or call 1-800-799-SAFE (7233).

One thing to remember should you access the site; no one will know you have been on it. It is automatically taken off the browsing history by the organization. They make sure to tell you this so that you know you are safe contacting them.

Cynthia can be found either writing on her laptop with her kitty "helping" or outside taking care of the flowers in the backyard. She enjoys reading, writing, meeting new people, learning new things, and most importantly, being one with nature. She enjoys spending time by the ocean or in the mountains.

Connect with Cynthia:

Website: https://www.personalwellnesscopywriter.com

LinkedIn: https://www.linkedin.com/cynthia-webster/

Facebook: https://www.facebook.com/profile.php?id=10001147082120

Instagram: https://www.instagram.com/cynthw363/

Email: webstercynthia090@gmail.com

One final thought: If you're able to, really listen to Lady Gaga's latest song, "Hold My Hand." She says, don't give up on yourself, and one day you'll be happy again.

CHAPTER 6

FERTILE GROUND

CULTIVATING SEEDS OF CHANGE

Gretchen Bruno, MD

"The only real prison, is in your mind."

~ Annetjie Roodt

MY STORY

Wrapped in a blanket of delicious sweat, I lay in the bliss of a well-earned savasana. My pulse, seemingly audible, echoed the tangible energy of the heated room. Rays of light danced through the windows, and a sense of movement remained, even as our bodies entered stillness.

My beloved yoga teacher, in his intoxicating South African accent and presence of a thousand stares, posed the question, "If you had three months to live, what would you change about your life?" The sting of my own tears transformed into a river, and my Highest Self cried out: My thoughts! My thoughts! I would change the way I think.

It would still be many years before I grasped the wisdom of that voice or had any ability to understand what that meant, but the seed was planted. I was fertile ground. All I needed was water to help it grow.

As life would have it, water is plentiful and comes in many forms. The question then becomes, how much water is enough?

* * *

With an unsteady gait and my heart in my throat, I walked down the stairs, stick in my hand. I caught my partner's eye as I neared the bottom step and simply held my hand out in front of me.

"That's it?!" he said in disbelief.

"That's it," I replied with a slight smile, fully realizing he was referring to the practice portion of babymaking.

The excitement of the possibilities ahead quickly shifted to the palpable dread and blanket of shame I still carried from the first time.

You're not fit to be a mother. I heard the distant voices of my family, now synonymous with my own.

We were much older than the societal norm for conceiving and certainly delightfully surprised by the matching pink line now that we had done things the "right" way, but the whispers of the past continued.

You can't even take care of yourself. How will you take care of a baby?

It didn't matter that I had been a physician for over ten years and achieved most of the adult milestones. I remembered all the times I needed their support and the indecision and terror I had with the first positive test.

Of course they said those things.

I quickly became the little girl who was perpetually afraid of what more they'd say. What I was beginning to understand, though, was that their words had simply been a reflection of the way I spoke to myself.

"We can't tell them. We can't tell anyone." I said.

"It's okay. We don't have to," he promised. "Not now. Not yet"

I will keep you safe little one. Please don't leave me this time. I said silently to my rapidly growing bundle of cells as we hugged and marveled at the idea of our new creation.

The cycle of shame and secrecy, though, continued. Flashbacks of the triangulated drama that ensued the year prior hit like lightning strikes, wrenching my stomach and throat into knots, leaving my body depleted and my mind anxious with all the familiar questions.

What if they're right? What if I am less capable than all the other women? What if I really am the one who is broken and wrong and not enough?

"I can do this, right?" I would ponder aloud.

"Of course, you can," he would say. "You're already an amazing mother."

For a brief moment, the buzz of anxiety would soften, but the cavern of doubt and insatiable need returned quickly with a vengeance.

Why can't you just make me feel better? Why don't you say the right things? If you had done things right in the first place, everything would be okay.

My surreptitious brain was always looking to the outside to fix whatever problem it was currently creating.

But no one could tell me the answers to my secret questions, the ones that haunted me since I was a little girl, so I set out to do what I know how to do best—control. This was known territory for me. Most of my life circled in this space, and I developed lots of ways of quieting the voices instead of feeling the pain.

Make things perfect.

There is an illusion of safety in the act of trying to control. I'd do everything right. I would prove I was enough. When things look good on the outside, you tend to attract approval.

Briefly, you think *I am okay.*

External glorification, achievements, and accolades, though, will never change the emptiness inside. It's an exhausting cycle of striving, achieving, judging, and striving again. The focus is on the outcome, not the process. When the outcome fails to reach perfection, as nothing ever can, the Self is punished, and the cycle begins again.

I know how to do this. I have to do this right.

I was going to be the best mother with the best pregnancy and the best delivery.

Of course, I didn't really know I was thinking these things at the time or even that the majority of my actions for much of my life were about controlling anxiety and escaping feelings, but they were. I was still very much caught in the idea that things and people outside of me were the cause of my feelings and actions. It had never occurred to me that I had a choice. I did not yet comprehend that I wasn't simply responding to external circumstances but instead responding to the unique monologue of my very own brain and how I was interpreting the outside.

Nevertheless, the Universe engaged my desperate and naive declaration of perfection with the blessing of a beautiful pregnancy. Other than the two days in the fetal position at 12 weeks trying to figure out how in the world I was going to be the mother of a little boy and the very brief scare that my cervix was too short and unable to keep my baby inside, things were effortless.

I loved my runs and swims and yoga sessions with my little buddy. We were a team, and I felt beautiful. I recall the day I realized the depth of my love for the soul who took up space in my rapidly growing body. I drove a road frequently traveled and had the slew of pictures from his first 3D ultrasound in my lap. I stopped at a light and looked at the picture of his profile, as I had done dozens of times before. Somehow, this time was different.

This little person is inside of me.

I created him.

He chose me.

A massive wave of gratitude enveloped me, and my body erupted with sobs of joy. *Thank you for coming to me, my sweet baby!*

My due date came and went. I still felt fabulous and knew my little person was just fine inside, but we tend to frown upon over 40s staying pregnant after their due date in obstetrics. The placenta gets tired, if you will, and the consequences are unspeakable, so I was strongly encouraged by my best friends and colleagues to come in for an induction.

This is not how it's supposed to go. What is wrong with my body?

The internal shame and judgment began.

I come from a line of women, both family and friends, who have exemplified the beauty and grace of labor and delivery at its finest. They were my role models and the ones I wanted to emulate and impress. I trained under midwives in residency who taught me how to deliver in any position to support a woman in natural, unmedicated labor. That is what I wanted. It was really all I would accept.

Apparently, that was not on the agenda for the highest growth of my soul.

After three days of being in the hospital, with very little progress, my best friend and physician entered the room.

"It's time Gretch," she said with an air of pity that made me want to scream.

Suddenly, this woman whom I love so very much became something else. Her voice echoed with unintelligible words in the "wah wah wah" of old cartoons.

The air of the hospital room grew even more sterile and cruel.

I knew, of course, what she was trying to say. I would not hear her. If I did, it would make it all real.

I said nothing but instead looked away with now rivers of grief from years of not enough exiting my body.

She left the room saying, "I will give you some time."

I looked at him through the thick film that only uncontrollable sobs can create. "We will not make it through this. If I have surgery, we will not be together." I warned as if somehow he had control over what was transpiring.

Instead of the reassurance I sought, he was stone-faced and silent, confirming my worst fears.

Damnit! Why can't you tell me it will all be okay. Why can't you tell me I'm amazing and beautiful and fully capable of being a mother no matter how our baby comes into this world? Why are you so absent and mean and dense? Why can't you answer all the questions?!

Instantly, I started reaching out to all the people whose approval I thought I needed to even breathe.

"Of course it's okay. It's what you need to bring this baby safely into the world," they all consoled.

That is not what my mind said.

What is wrong with you? Everyone else can do this. Why isn't he coming? Of course, the one thing you need to prove you are worthy is the one thing they won't give you time to do. This is what's wrong with doctors. They don't care. They don't listen. They don't know. This is going to ruin my child. I'm already a bad mother, and he isn't even here.

Remember, I'm a physician. I've been the one on the other side. There is no right way to have a baby, and mothers come in many forms. None of what my mind said made sense, but that didn't matter. Worthless and inept infiltrated my core.

Hours later, I conceded our fate. The walk to the operating room was, for me, a walk of shame in the deepest sense. I had failed, and I hadn't even begun.

As cesarean sections go, however, mine was as crunchy and spiritual as you could make it. We played my carefully curated birth playlist made by one of my wisest and dearest friends. We soaked wet cloths with my birth oils and placed them around my head. And magically, the room was filled with unending love and laughter from people who respected and adored me and wanted both patients on the table to be happy and healthy. Thankfully, I did let go of the terrible voice inside, chastising me for the ways I'd failed, and got ready to meet the amazing boy I had grown inside my body.

"My baby, my baby, my baby," I cried as he was victoriously placed directly on my chest, breaking all sterile technique that is generally accepted in the operating room. This amazing being was now with me on a whole different level. His little arms reached, grasping at my flesh with sweet, triumphant cries signifying he was, indeed, okay.

I breathed in the enrapturing scent and presence of my newborn and smiled an exhausted but eternally grateful smile. The sting of my self-made failure seemed worlds away for a time.

The real journey, however, had just begun.

"I hope you like it here, sweet boy," I said as we walked through the door with the now consistent tears that sat ready to erupt at any moment.

Postpartum is hard. Breastfeeding is hard. It will challenge even the most secure with the hint of not-enoughness we all fear deep inside.

What if I'm not really his mother because he wasn't birthed through my vagina? What if his real mother comes and takes him away from me?

I didn't talk about my delivery. I couldn't even surmise allowing the word C-section to exit my lips. I let people believe what they wanted. I never corrected or discussed it. I simply let them marvel at the universal beauty of new life. I continued to hide and stew in my thoughts in between the vast majority of time spent simply learning how to take care of a baby.

I can't go back to work. What will they think? My patients won't take me seriously. My colleagues will laugh at me.

The voices get quieter over time and find something else to talk about, but their overall message is the same no matter the circumstance. We all have our own birth stories, whether they're related to birth or not. If we pay attention, we start recognizing the pattern and have endless opportunities to become curious.

Wait a minute. Is this true?

Beliefs are just thoughts we think repeatedly. Thoughts are not facts.

I knew my thoughts were unfounded in so many ways, but I accepted them as fact for so, so long. I'd never put such shameful and detrimental thoughts on another human being, especially about how they birthed their child, but somehow, my brain thought it was okay to do that to myself.

What if I could choose a different thought? What if this isn't about the birth at all? What if nothing has gone wrong? What if I am not a perfect mother but the perfect mother for my son? What if all the answers are within?

And suddenly, germination begins. The water has finally permeated the ground.

When you start to believe something could be different, you'll start to see evidence supporting your supposition. The series of serendipitous events and realizations that led me to thought work took years. In the middle of life coach training, something clicked. I realized, while listening to Eckhart Tolle, that coaching was the bridge between all the teachings I loved and day-to-day life. It was the link between the wisdom of thought leaders and the possibilities in our own lives. It was a way not to escape feeling, but to understand the origination of feeling, to honor feelings, permission and courage to feel feelings, and the option to choose thoughts that could even create new and different feelings. It was the ability to tell a different story—one that serves and uplifts rather than shames and minimizes. It was the opportunity to heal, create, and become the Self that is underneath our cultural conditioning and the inaccurate conclusions of childhood.

The seedling grew.

My desire is to share this simple wisdom with you. I aspire to give you tools that can help you become aware of what you're thinking that's leading you to your feelings and results and empower you to see and create new possibilities in your own life. I invite you to practice with me and am honored you made it this far.

THE PRACTICE

Make a commitment to yourself.

Find a comfortable seat every morning or evening with the purpose of reflection.

Write down as many thoughts as you can identify, stream of consciousness. You can choose thoughts about a particular circumstance or simply thoughts you're having in general.

Remember, circumstances are facts that everyone in the room could agree upon. For example, He said, "these words." We then get to choose our thoughts about what was said.

"He is mean or uncaring or obnoxious or amazing" is a thought and not fact.

Find the thought with the most emotional charge or the one that seems the most prevalent. This may seem overwhelming at first. Remember, we think at least 60,000 thoughts a day, and most of them are negative. Allow.

If you come up with "I don't know what I am thinking," be gentle with yourself and understand this is the brain's way of keeping you safe (i.e., stuck, confused). Ask yourself, "But what if I did know?"

Allow yourself to think about the thought and identify the feeling that is coming from that thought.

Find the feeling in your body. Name it. Give it color, texture, and space. Breathe into the feeling and watch to see if it changes. Remember, you are safe. Feelings are simply vibrations in our bodies. We are safe to feel.

From the feeling that has arisen from your thought, surmise your actions or inactions and ultimately the results that particular thought and feeling combination are creating in your life.

Write it all down.

Watch with curiosity and compassion. Whatever you are thinking and feeling and doing and creating is okay.

Sometimes, we cannot choose a different thought until we have processed and deescalated the thought and feeling we're in. You cannot always choose a different belief until the power has been removed from the current one. Power is lost in identification and assimilation.

Recognize your power. See what you've created. Start to become familiar with your thoughts throughout the day.

This practice can become an adjunct to meditation. Identifying something as a thought quiets the chaos around it.

When you're ready to create, decide on your new, intentional thought. You must practice this thought with such dedication that you can embody the feeling created by the thought. Pay attention to thoughts you have about yourself. Your results will never surpass your self-perception. Understand that, as you hold your focus and internalize something emotionally, you will shift the results you see in your life.

Believe it, and you will see it!

I am **Gretchen Bruno,** MD, a dedicated physician, passionate life coach, grateful mama, and perpetual student of life. I have practiced OBGyn in Denver, Colorado, since 2004 and have greatly enjoyed cultivating the ability to hold space for women from all backgrounds. A long-time yogi and novice meditator, I also enjoy triathlon, skiing, and walks with our new puppy. I have been on a journey of self-discovery for as long as I can remember. Yoga teacher training, Ironman races, and meditation retreats were some of my favorites on the path to learning how I work and up-leveling my life, but ultimately, coaching and understanding what is underneath my emotions, actions, and results have shifted my life immeasurably in terms of what I now know to be possible. I help midlife women caught in the chaos of a societally prescribed life awaken, transform, and create the second half they envision. Reach out! I'd love to talk.

Connect with Gretchen:

Website: www.gretchenbrunomd.com

CHAPTER 7

NAVIGATING PAST THE NEGATIVITY

BREAKING THE CYCLE OF CHILDHOOD TRAUMA

Karen Rosenfeld Montgomery

MY STORY

Dinner time at my house was always a real treat (That's sarcasm). I thought my mother was mentally ill or she was having some sort of breakdown. Or she was just batshit crazy. It didn't matter what the reason was. It was fucked up. She was like an unstable missile, and for whatever reason, I was the target—always at the dinner table.

There were plenty of other times too, but this one you could set your watch to. On any given evening at 6:00 p.m., the same scenario ensued. My family sat in our tiny kitchen, my father at the head of the table. The opposite end of the table was against the wall under the window. My older brother Dave and I sat next to each other, and I was in the corner. My mom and younger brother sat on the other side.

The seating is essential to the story, so keep that in mind.

So, dinner starts. "Pass the potatoes, don't eat the legs; they are for the baby! Don't eat the wings; they are for Dave!" *Holy shit, woman. We know exactly what parts of the chicken go to who.* Even in my eight-year-old brain, I knew this was ridiculous.

Then something happened. I don't know what triggered it. I don't think anything specific. A smart-mouth comment, perhaps? A laugh that was probably louder than she liked? There was no telling why, but something flipped a switch in her, setting off a symphony of thundering sounds accompanied by a tornado of wrathful fury. She started banging her hands on the table. Everyone stopped eating. The silverware rattled. The dishes shook. The water in our drinking glasses rippled with waves. We were all about to be in the eye of my mother's storm.

Then came the screaming. That was Dave's cue to push himself in as close to the table as he could. I could see him doing it from the corner of my left eye. He was making room for me to make my escape. Just as my mother's anger exploded into full-blown rage, I squeezed behind my brother, ran through the dining and living rooms, and ran for my life up the stairs as she tried to catch me. I flew into the bathroom, closing and locking the door with one motion as I did so many times before. I caught my breath as I sat on the side of the bathtub feeling safe, even though she was banging on the door, still screaming. But she couldn't get to me. I was locked in. I would wait it out. She would cool off, and it would be over.

More than once, she was so upset about the state of my bedroom that she wiped her arm violently across my dresser like a deranged lunatic. I watched in horror as all of my treasures fell to the floor in a crash, and my heart broke right along with everything else. Whenever she screamed in my face with such force and volume that I wished she'd just hit me, no one was there to protect me. I didn't enjoy that part either, but the screaming was somehow worse. So many times, I sat alone in my bedroom and sobbed after something like that happened. I can still remember that feeling of pure despair.

In the middle and late seventies, when I was a kid, Child Protective Services wasn't getting called for mental abuse. They weren't coming every time my mother commented on how fat I was or how she always stifled me any time I tried to have a voice. Nor did a fairy godmother abruptly pop up in a cloud of glitter to give me a Xanax and explain that all that fuckery and negativity was setting me up for an adulthood of self-loathing. Mental abuse would rob me of self-confidence and cripple me from pursuing a successful education or career. Because I felt undeserving, I did not allow the right men into my life. Making simple decisions about anything without questioning myself became nearly impossible.

Then there was the mind fuck. Usually, after my mother lost her shit on me, she returned to my bedroom in tears. She apologized and wanted a hug and a kiss. *Fucking really?*

I did it. I hugged and kissed her. I felt terrible for her. It was clear to me, even then, that something inside my mother was wrong. I loved her, but I hated her with every fiber of my being. There was no therapist to explain what my mother didn't even understand. I knew at a very young age that if I ever had children, I'd never treat them like this. I'd be the person my child needed when they were hurting. I'd choose acceptance, compassion, and patience.

I would break the cycle.

My mother was born in 1942. Times were different then. Men and women played specific roles, and my grandfather played the role of asshole, abusive father, and husband. My mom never talked about any specifics except one story about a cat-of-nine-tails. A cat-of-nine-tails is a multi-tailed whip that originated as an implement for severe physical punishment. Why the fuck would a person even have one of these? And where would a person acquire one? Do you think he just woke up one morning and was like, *I'm sick of my wife and two daughters pissing me off, so after I have my coffee, I think I will go down to ye olde whip shop and get me one of those behavior tamers?*

No one knows where it came from. My mom only knows that it hung on the back of a door.

Until it didn't.

My mother's sister is nine years older. At the age of 18, my grandfather insisted that she get married, and she was pissed about it. She was so angry, in fact, that she wouldn't allow her father to walk her down the aisle. That's pretty bold for an 18-year-old girl in 1951. She made one other gutsy move. After she was married, she came back to the house for a visit with a purpose. While she was there, she found that cat-of-nine-tails and cut it up into tiny pieces. She did what she could to save my mother from the wrath of the whip.

I've heard that story so many times. My aunt was a hero that day, and that day lives on in my mother's mind even now. My mom, 80, and her sister, 89.

I believe we learn our lessons when it's time, and it'll take as long as it takes. It took me having a baby and about ten years of marriage to my husband, who suffered greatly from alcoholism, for me to see things clearly. Honestly, it took his death for the clarity to come. I became a widow at 48; my husband Mitchell was 52. Our beautiful daughter was nine.

Addiction is a horrible, debilitating thing. The three of us were on a journey full of bumps, twists, turns, rehabs, disappointments, and a few triumphs. But ultimately, when a human abuses their body the way he did, God bless him and his sweet soul; no one could survive that. And he did not.

A few years before that, we three moved into my parents' house due to a job change and relocation back to my hometown. It was really a miracle and the answer to my prayers. I think I manifested it to happen. Because of my work schedule, I left my then three-year-old daughter with my drunk husband for eight-hour shifts every weekend for a year and a half. It was unbearable to my soul. My life was stressful, complicated, and sucked. It fucking sucked. I didn't know what I was supposed to do.

You know, people don't always understand how complicated things are for other people. Even people that know you well. I felt like I was stuck. I had a lease. I was married. I had a job. I was trying to keep my little family together. I felt hopeless. Then, one evening Mitch got a phone call. He was invited back to work for a previous employer. It wasn't a company he wanted to work for again, but I didn't give a shit. "You are taking this job no matter what," I told him. I was able to transfer back home with the company I worked for, and I was relieved. The universe heard me. I needed my mom. And there it was.

We moved in with my parents. My father was elderly and not well. It was important to me that my daughter got to know him at least a little bit before he was gone. My mother kept him alive with love and saltless food that he hated. There was laughter and security in my childhood home. Life felt better.

Things between my husband and I were rocky, of course. It's extremely difficult to deal with all the bullshit that comes with a person who is drunk every day. My mother and I were on the same page there. It was nice to finally have her support. But not everything was good. I saw my mom scream like an animal in my five-year-old's face like she used to do to me when I was a child. I pounced like a mother in the wild, retrieving her baby from prey. I let that woman have it. "Take your hands off of her! You will never, ever touch her or scream at her like that again, do you hear me?" I was loud. My blood was boiling. My daughter ran into my bedroom and was on my bed, crying. It was deja vu. *I can't believe I'm in my childhood bedroom watching my own daughter suffer from this. It's like I'm watching myself. I can't believe I put her in this situation.*

I held my baby close and wiped her tears away. "I'm so sorry, my baby. Sometimes Bubbie is very mean. At least she's just your Grandmother and not your mother," I said as tears streamed down my face. She looked at me then. I could see that she understood exactly what I said. I saw empathy in my daughter's face. She understood my pain because she was feeling it at that very moment. And I cried. We cried together.

It took a long time for me to understand my mother and longer to accept the way she is. She was dealt a pretty shitty hand growing up, and I know she was always doing the best she could for us. It wasn't all hideous. She wasn't and isn't without humor or love. I know she loved me and loves me still. She loves all of us. And she loved my father. Everyone loved my father.

My dad was, and I truly believe this, the single best person to ever walk this Earth. He had a mentally abusive father, but he wasn't wired like my mom is, I guess.

I used to have secret meetings with him where I asked him why he married her. He wouldn't even entertain an answer. I mean, how would you answer that as a parent in 1979? You wouldn't. You would stay strong and not say anything negative about your spouse to your child. Besides, what could he say? He didn't know.

He's been gone seven years now. That's seven years my family has had broken hearts. My parents were married for 50 years.

I'm 50 years old now. My mom is 80. She just sold the house I grew up in. Just two days ago, in fact. FYI, that bathroom I used to lock myself in still has the original door. The lock no longer works, and you can push the door open with one finger. A lot of shit went down in that house. But that's life, isn't it? I know I painted a pretty ugly little glimpse of a tiny blip into my childhood, but it's one of many unpleasant truths. Life happened there. It's because she was selling the house that all of this childhood trauma has come up for me. I buried a lot of it for a really long time. I love my mother. I want to poke her in the eye a lot of the time, but I love my mother. She has a story, too. Every person has a story. Every person has reasons for the things they do. They might be completely fucked up reasons, and there may be some deep wounds that people don't even know they have.

The night after Thanksgiving 2019, at 9:45 p.m., the doorbell rang. *Who the fuck is at the door?* My husband wasn't home. He must have had his keys. *Why the doorbell?* I looked out the little window into the dark; there were two police officers. I knew what this was. Mitch was dead. My first thought was, *Oh God, he was drunk driving and killed a family.* I turned on the outside light and opened the door. He did pass away. It was a blood clot. He was at the gym.

End scene.

Drop the curtain.

Shortly after my husband died, I received a call through Facebook Messenger from my friend Jennifer McCauley, who I hadn't seen in over 30 years. It was a call that changed my life. She is possibly the most spiritual person I have ever spoken to. Jennifer told me so much information during that phone call that I was overcome with a sense of calm and also excitement. I had an understanding of things I had never heard of before. I was enlightened. I felt hopeful for the first time in almost a decade. When we got off the phone, I, of course, immediately forgot everything she told me, except for one thing. "Give your ancestors permission to help you," she said. That sounded good to me. I needed a new way to find some healing. It was exactly what I needed, and it was something I could do.

At that time in 2019, I was still smoking cigarettes, and given the circumstances, I wasn't planning on quitting anytime soon. It was December in central New York, and it was freezing, but I didn't care. I headed out to the garage after dinner for my evening cigarette, or two, or five, or ten. It was a thing, and I was just doing my thing. I was sitting in one of those folding camping chairs, garage door open, smoking and looking out at the dark sky. I wasn't sure how much of what I was exhaling was smoke and how much of it was my breath into the cold night air. I was playing casino games on my phone, trying and succeeding in losing myself. I looked up from my phone into the outdoors. I put the phone into the cupholder of my chair. I stood up and went outside into the front yard. I looked up at the starry sky for a long moment. It was quiet. I was quiet. I allowed my mind to be quiet. Then I threw my hands up into the air and said out loud with a full heart, *"Ancestors! I give you permission to help me! Please. Please help me."* I cried, tears streaming down my face beneath and beyond my fabulous glasses, making a little thud each time a drop fell onto my coat.

Things started to fall into place after that. I don't know if it works just because it works, or more likely that I believe in it. And why not? Saying this, I feel good. It gives me a place to put my gratitude.

It's two and a half years later. My daughter is 12. We live in our own home. There is no yelling or screaming. There is no hitting. Negative comments are never said to one another. There is encouragement and understanding. My daughter goes to therapy every week, and she is happy to go. We have our issues, of course, but we respect those things about each other.

I continue to give my ancestors permission to help me. Sometimes I just say, *Thank you for continuing to help me in my life. Thank you for my home! Thank you for my daughter! Thank you for my life. Thank you for helping me find clarity and peace.* I give my ancestors permission to help me show love for my mother. She's been through her own share of problems. So has my sweet daughter. So have I. So have we all.

None of us are without struggle. It's up to us to find compassion. Find that compassion for yourself. You need it most.

THE PRACTICE

1. Find a place where you can be alone, anywhere (outside, garage, in your car, home, etc.).

2. Put your hands up in the air and say, **"Ancestors! I give you permission to help me! Please. Please help me."** Say this as many times as you need.

3. Trust that your ancestors are listening, guiding, and helping you.

I truly hope this practice helps you as much as it has helped me.

Karen Rosenfeld Montgomery is a widow and a mother of one daughter, living in Syracuse, New York. Karen is a dog lover, an artist, and a writer. She enjoys writing her blog on Tumblr—*The Life of Karen*—a funny and sometimes serious but always real place to find inspiration. Karen loves to cook and entertain in her home and spends as much time with family and friends as possible. She looks forward to many more exciting writing projects in the near future.

CHAPTER 8

HOW TO SURVIVE AND NAVIGATE LIFE

AFTER THE DEATH OF A TEENAGE CHILD

Pamela D. Jordan, MAJ, US Army

MY STORY

"What did you just say? Hello? I thought I heard you say cancer. Is that what you said? Hold on, let me get off the highway." Waves of confusion entered my head as my husband was talking.

Clearly, they're mistaken. Kids don't get cancer just like that. My head and eyes shifted back and forth as I tried to find somewhere to park.

"The doctor's been trying to reach us all day, Pam. I think your phone was off? Christien's MRI from this morning came back. They said he has cancer. They're almost 100% sure. They need to do a biopsy, but the doctor wants us to take him to McLane's Children's in the morning."

"Pam, are you listening to me?"

What the Fuck? I don't understand what is happening—not my child. *There must be a mistake.*

"Okay, I'm still here. I'm just really confused. The last time Christien was seen, the physician's assistant said it was growing pains because he was getting taller. This doesn't make any sense. I don't understand." I took a deep breath. "Healthcare is not an exact science. It's a mistake. We'll get this figured out." My military thinking started kicking in. Staring at the time, I realized it was 7 p.m. "I need to call my Colonel."

"Hi Sir, really sorry to disturb you, but I have an emergency. No, Sir, nothing with the company. It's my family. Um, I don't know how to say this, but, um, ah, well. . ."

"Just say it, Captain Jordan. Don't worry about calling. What's the emergency?"

"Sir, it's my son Christien. He had an MRI earlier today, and the doctor was trying to reach us earlier and. . ."

"Yes, I remember you mentioning your son's appointment earlier today, Pam. What is it?"

"Sir, they said he has cancer. He has cancer in his knee."

"Are they sure? Oh my goodness, I am so sorry."

"I think so. We have to take Christien to McLane's in the morning. They will be waiting for us."

"Okay, take care of your son Pam. We will cover for you. Don't worry about anything. I will be praying for Christien tonight."

Somehow, saying it out loud to the boss sounded so surreal. I sound like I'm giving a report. What the hell is wrong with me? Shouldn't I be more frantic? God! This is my fucking child!

Oh shit. I could feel acid inching its way up my throat. Breathe Pam, and drink some water. I'm flustered, looking through my bag for my water. "Where is it?!" My voice escalated at no one, smashing the steering and the dash. My chest tightened, my breath shortened, and sweat dripped down my face as the heat started to take over my entire body, which shook from its core. Breathe, breathe, breathe. Take a deep breath and focus.

Get it together, Pam. C'mon, girl, remain calm. You got this.

I can't let Christen see me like this. *WooSah Woosah Whooooosaaaahhhh. . .*

I looked around, unaware of my surroundings, and realized I had pulled into a church parking lot. Ah, fitting place, but time to go home. God is in control, and tomorrow morning, those doctors will say that they made a mistake and it's a miracle that Christien doesn't have cancer.

Please, God, work your miracles; if anyone is healed in your name, it will be Christien.

I stopped to pick up dinner and then headed home. I turned onto my street; my heart started racing. My hands gripped the steering wheel as I pulled into the garage and noticed Christien's light was on. I started thinking about what to say when I walked inside. Stay calm, no stressing, focus on God and miracles, and approach this like the common cold.

Entering the house I announced, "What does everyone want for dinner? I have Mexican!" Although the corners of my mouth were up, my jaw was tighter than an alligator's grip.

Upon our arrival to the PEDS HEMOC clinic I was taken aback—there were at least 8 people in the room. "We are 99% sure the tumor has grown out of the bone and infected his tissue." The Orthopedic surgeon, explained. *Wow, he's really young for a surgeon! Does he even know what he's talking about?*

"This is textbook, but it is so progressed we need to get it out like yesterday!" Shit, trying to stay in control, my body became light and tingly, and my breath shortened. I was afraid I'd fall to the ground.

I did not train for this! I have gone through extensive military training, but I'm not ready to deal with a situation I have no control over. I feel nauseous. The doctor began to talk about Christien's treatment Master Protocol (MAP) medications. I knew he was talking because his lips were moving, but I'm not processing anything past "biopsy." Not anything. Was I losing my hearing?

"We need to schedule Christien to get a biopsy very soon." I feel numb and like crying. I want to scream, but the sound just won't come out. I will embarrass myself here. I wonder how I'm supposed to respond? I feel my head moving up and down like I understand what the doctor is telling me.

Fake it till you make it, Pam, fake it till you make it. "And pray," I whispered.

Staring at Christien, his sweet face is in shock and scared. I can tell, like me, he doesn't understand what is happening. I turn to look at my husband, for reassurance I guess. His eyes were locked on the floor. I guess he's also looking baffled, so the oncologists are looking at me for a response. So what?! Am I supposed to say something? Have questions? I don't really know what to say!

I look at my child from the corner of my eye as I start to take notes, a natural approach from being in the military. I don't know what to say to him, but I hope I'm mimicking the calmness and strength I think he's gonna need for this battle ahead.

I know diddly squat about cancer, but I will fake it till I make it because my son's life depends on it. Shit, I fight for folks I don't know. Now I need to fight for mine! Literally!

I'm efficiently plugging in dates to work my schedule around his treatments as I have an internal battlefield in my mind. As a Caribbean immigrant, I look and sound very different from others. Finding a seat at the table while at the same time stroking the egos of men of all races and at the same time fighting off the females, who have the Queen Bee complex, can be exhausting. It's like you're always being judged. Heck, I just took Company Command, a position I fought for three years to get. I could lose it if I'm not present. I must figure out how to save my son without being removed from command.

"Let's get him scheduled for the biopsy and chemo," the lead oncologist chimed in. "The sooner we start, the best chance he has. We will also schedule him for the limb salvage surgery?"

It's been two weeks since Christien's biopsy and starting chemo. I couldn't remember his treatment master protocol medications for my life, but like the smart kid Christien was, he recalled.

Oh my God, I can't with this kid; he's so funny! Constantly quizzing the nurses on "the poison" they were pumping into him through the IV (his words, not mine).

"And what is Methotrexate supposed to do? What is the drip rate? Should I press the bell if I'm itching, or is that a normal side effect. Can I have cookies with that?"

I swiftly gave the nurse the side-eye and caught Christien giggling. Of course, he wanted a reaction out of me because I strictly monitor his sugar intake. But, unfortunately, cancer likes sweets, and he was to have little to none.

Two years into Christien's treatment, I walked into an ambush when I was visiting him and bringing his lunch.

"Hi, Baby! Here's your Chic-Fil-A. Wanna eat now or. . ."

Christien snappily interrupted, "Mom, it's been two years, and I still have cancer.

"Look at me! Look at me! I hate this—I'm hating this! I want my life back! When will this stop? I didn't do anything to nobody! I have been kind. I have been good! I have prayed! God is not listening to my prayers! God has abandoned me!"

My heart crumbled hearing these words come out of my son's mouth. I tried to remain as composed as best as I could. "What happened? I was just on the phone asking you what you want to eat and. . . what happened?"

I looked at the nurse for an answer, and she was wiping away tears as she exited Christien's room.

"*Cálmate*. . .shhh. . .shh, *mi amor* (calm down, my love), what happened? Where is this coming from? Did the doctor visit you?"

"Yes. I don't wanna talk, Mom." His tone softened. "Why is God not answering my prayers. Am I saying the wrong prayer? Am I not worth saving? Why is he punishing me? Every time I get a little better, something else happens. Maybe I am not worth saving, and he's sending the message, and we are just not listening, Mom. I just want this to be over. You said God would work miracles for me. This can't be a miracle because miracles shouldn't hurt! Besides, he's not listening."

Christien is angry, and his outburst is heartbreaking. His puffy, sunburned eyes from chemo were full of tears, and he started to cry uncontrollably. I moved closer and tried to hug him, knowing he couldn't wipe the tears that would sting the chemo-burnt skin around his eyes. "Don't, Mom, just don't. Even my skin hurts."

Through his tears, he asked me to turn the lights off and close the blinds. "I just wanna rest for a bit."

I was sitting on the couch watching Christien sleep. I had the same questions. Why was God not interceding? I couldn't help that nagging thought that somehow, this was my fault.

I recalled telling a group of parents at a gymnastics event for my daughter, "If I were to lose all my kids, Christien is the one special child I could not do without. He's the most selfless, loving angel here on Earth."

Less than a year after I said that Christien was battling cancer. That didn't stop his thoughtfulness and desire to help others. Because we loved stopping at Starbucks before appointments and hospitalizations, Chris came up with the "Pay it forward times two." He looked in the side view mirror and asked me to pay for the orders of two to three cars behind us (if it was within budget) and, in turn, ask them to pay it forward for the cars behind them. With excitement, he wrote notes on napkins requesting they pay the gift forward (This is a gift from Christien M. Quiles. Please play along and pay it forward in honor of my fight against Osteosarcoma - Childhood Bone Cancer)

Now here we are. My angel is dying with no miracle in sight.

I couldn't blame Christien. He did nothing to deserve this. We made light of the situation, trying always to have faith and hope because cancer strips you of everything good. Your looks, your life, your dignity, it takes it all.

Months later, I overheard Christien talking and pleading with God in the shower to heal him. Again, I felt helpless hearing my kid, now 16, begging God to spare his life.

One of the things I learned from Christien was not to be afraid to try new things. In addition to being a soldier, I became a social media influencer because of him.

He would say, "Mom, you do everything for me and haven't been doing anything for yourself. I know you will love it. Just let me do it for you. I know you will love it."

Christien created a YouTube account and channel for me while I was at work. I literally cried with joy when I saw how happy he was to show me what he had created. I nervously filmed my first video on YouTube that day.

All these memories. My baby fought valiantly, yet cancer kept coming back. He fought to attend classes, play in his upright bass in concert, attend his prom, and walk across the stage to receive his diploma. He is my hero!

Osteosarcoma painfully spread to Christien's spine and throughout his body, and his lungs filled with fluid in real time. Then, three months to the day after he graduated high school, Christien died.

I felt like I had died with my son. Caring for him for almost four years consumed my life. My priorities were Christien, work, my family, and then me. Christien's death created a massive breakdown in my family.

I was detached and did not want to live, and I'm still struggling with his death to this day, trying to do more than exist.

My living kids were 25, 13, and two when Christien died, and they're still trying to deal with his loss. Now I'm trying to mend and improve communications between myself and my family and make myself a priority.

I'm still angry at myself. I'm angry at God. I'm angry and have nowhere to place this anger that's making me physically ill. Can my heart ever be mended?

Well, now that I've expunged all the pent-up nasty feelings and taste of bile from my stomach and lungs—what do I do? Maybe I should just let the tears flow. But I also struggle with imposter syndrome (pretending to be okay when I'm not); therefore, I've had to work even harder to not become emotionless. I've learned to trust my instincts, surround myself with supportive friends, and continue to do unexpected things that bring my life joy, and most importantly, I've learned to let go.

The pain doesn't go away, but it becomes a realm I can navigate within as opposed to being crippled by.

How does that work, though, considering I am an emotional woman? It doesn't. But I attempt to review problems beyond the obvious and move past the hurt.

I would love to guide you on practices that have helped in my healing. These practices can help if you've lost a child/children, parent, sibling, family member or if there is someone you want to keep close to your heart.

THE PRACTICE

- **Learn to trust your instincts.** When I have the worst time with people or situations, I don't heed my instincts. **Don't do that!** I looked for mentorship and sisterhood and got constant disappointment when I didn't heed my instincts.

- **Make new friends** with new interests (Online friends count, too). Some real-life folks don't always know how to cultivate a friendship.

- **Do something unexpected** to bring joy to someone else. As previously mentioned, something as little as 'paying it forward' helps me feel like I am contributing.

- **Protect your energy** by making decisions that are good for you before they are suitable for others (only).

- **Let go.** Don't be afraid to let go. If you're always the one calling, texting, or visiting, you may need to release the relationship. Stop it. It hurts, but do you really need to be in that space? People who value you will reach out to you.

  After Christien died, people scattered to the four winds. Some haven't called or messaged me in the almost 6 years since he's died. I remember after his funeral service, I wondered how many people would travel to my funeral service. But then, I realized just my family and maybe a few friends I could count on one hand.

- **Pursue something new.** I always wanted to be a broadcaster when I was little, but I gave up that dream until Christien convinced me to create a Youtube channel.

  He badgered me, "Mom, you should do a video when we get back. I can create your channel for you, so you have no excuse." I'm broadcasting all over the world on my own channel now!

- **Create a nonprofit or volunteer** with one. I created a nonprofit in honor of Christien. This gave me a sense of purpose like I'm living his legacy to help others.

- **Consider a career change.** It's empowering when you take a chance on yourself! You are not meant to stay in the same space forever!

  I want to spend more time with my kids and my husband and travel more. I no longer have that sense of pride I once had. Plus, I'm tired and want to be free to be me, free to live the life my son was unable to, in his memory and his honor.

I miss you, Christien.

Love, your Momma.

Pam Jordan

Major, United States Army

Pam is an active-duty officer in the United States Army. Serving in the Medical Services for over 30 years in clinical and administrative capacities. She is married with four children, GyllMichael, Christien, Elyssa, and Nathan, and two fur babies, Arthur and Missy.

Pam is a Fragrance and Lifestyle Influencer. She is actively engaged on Instagram, YouTube, and TikTok platforms, where she shares her reviews with over 12K followers.

Pam also hosts fundraising events to bring awareness to Osteosarcoma and to assist with Osteosarcoma Research. Collaborating with MIB Agents to form a nonprofit in her son's memory—The Christien Quiles Osteosarcoma Research Fund.

Pam chills out by spending time with her family, creating content, and traveling. She also enjoys lying by the pool with a glass of wine.

Connect with Pam:

EMAIL: pamfam20@gmail.com

INSTAGRAM: @_pamjordan
http://www.instagram.com/_pamjordan/

TIKTOK: @thepamjordan

YOUTUBE: Pam Jordan _ Pam Fam
https://www.youtube.com/c/PamJordanPamFAM

FACEBOOK: Pam Jordan
https://www.facebook.com/pam.jordan.3363

CHAPTER 9

I AM WORTHY

TO BE LOVED AND ADORED BY SOMEONE

Tanya Stokes

MY STORY

I was so careful. I didn't see any signs. However, the longer I thought it out, I have to admit all the signs were there. I found out the man I was in a relationship with was married. I felt like a sucker. I thought I did all I was supposed to do. I took my time this go around. I got to know him. Well, I thought I did. Mr. Man met my kids, was in my home, and met key people in my life. He even had a key to my house!

After an hour and a half drive home, I sat in my car in my driveway, digging deep to find the strength not to cry, but you know I did. The tears fell and flowed like an uncontrollable river after several days of rain. They wracked my body as I rocked back and forth and from side to side. I boo-hoo'd until my nose started running and blowing bubbles. While searching for tissues, I hiccupped only once, thank God, wiped my face, and blew my nose. I'm one ugly sistah when I cry. I walked through my door and slammed it. The house shook from the blow.

Immediately my daughter ran down the steps. Her big brown eyes opened wide with a look of concern on her face. "Mommy, what's wrong?

Why are you crying?" In my mind: *Now, Tanya, you done scared the poor girl. You need to do better.* I looked straight into her eyes and said forcefully through clenched teeth, "Never allow anyone to tell you or make you feel or believe that you don't deserve to be treated like the queen you are." I kissed her gently on her forehead and went to my room, leaving her looking at the back of my body, dazed and confused. I heard her whisper, "Where did that come from?" I stayed in my room for the remainder of the night, replaying the events of the day over and over. They wouldn't go away no matter what I tried.

On that day, I received a phone call from Mr. Man's wife. Yeah, you heard me, his wife. When I picked up the phone, I heard, "Hello, Tanya?" and I answered, "Hello." The caller said, "This is Yolanda, Mr. Man's wife." My heart's rhythm skipped a beat before increasing rapidly while I processed this new information. *This has got to be a joke.*

She continued, "It has come to my attention that you have been seeing my husband for some time now. By the way, you're not the only one I've had this conversation with. He must have feelings for you because you've lasted longer than the others." She chuckled on the phone. I was about to answer, but she continued without taking a breath. "Well, I just wanted you to know you can have him because I'm divorcing his ass." I was about to say something again, but all I heard was a dial tone. I was in shock and annoyed at the same time.

This altercation took me back to when I was going through my divorce. It was one of the hardest life-changing events in my life. My mind, body, and soul went through changes I don't wish on anyone. My ex-husband wasn't the kindest of men. He was controlling, selfish, and abusive. To be told, "No one will want you with all these kids," by the man I was married to for 13 years was a punch in the gut. I lost myself during those 13 years with him. He robbed me of my youthful years. My spirit was crushed. My mental state deteriorated and continued on a downward spiral.

My self-esteem was at an all-time low. I felt like I wasn't good enough to do my job. I began making silly mistakes. *I don't have what it takes to be a good wife or a good mother. My husband no longer sees me as a help mate. He no longer has anything positive to say about me or to me. He has turned on me, and now he wants a divorce.* I expected him to want to take my children from me. My stomach turned flips every day. Food no longer pleased me.

My appetite was gone. However, I forced myself to eat because I had to remain healthy for my kids.

My appearance no longer interested me. *I mean, I haven't been looking my best at all. My hair looks like a wilderness area. My clothes are clean, but they might match and some days they don't. I wear what is quick and obtainable. Sometimes I wear the same outfit three times in one week. That has never been me. I am ashamed of myself.*

I believed and bought into everything my ex-husband said. For years I felt like I didn't deserve to be happy, cared for, or pampered. I didn't deserve to have my own cheerleader in my corner supporting me, my dreams, or aspirations. I thought my role was to satisfy the man, and as long as he was satisfied, I was good. Turns out that was not the play. He led me to believe I shouldn't ask him to do anything for me. He brought home the money and gave me what he wanted to contribute to the household. Since we did not discuss finances, this led me to work two jobs to make up the slack. This did not stop him from asking me what was for dinner as soon as I stepped into the house.

No matter what I did, it didn't satisfy him, especially sexually. I tried everything in the bedroom. My desire to please him appeared to bring out his meanness and desire to criticize and hurt me while destroying my womanhood. If I timidly asked about his feelings after sex, he would tell me, "I've had better," as he got out of bed to shower, dress, and leave the house. This psychological warfare destroyed me. I didn't know what to do or how to react. I sank deeper into depression.

I thought I asked all the right questions. Mr. Man presented himself as being kind, gentle, and attentive. I thought I hit the jackpot. Catering to my every need and supporting me financially, physically, and mentally, he knew what to say to get me to back down when I started asking too many questions. His reply would be, "You need to relax." I can't stand it when someone says that to me.

As I started thinking back on our relationship, I was able to pick up on the inconsistencies of little things. For example, not answering the phone at certain times of the day, not coming to visit me because I live "Too damn far." I live 35 minutes away on a no-traffic day. Our outings were always out of the area, never anything close to his home, or mine for that matter. I never met any of his family, can you believe that? The closest I got was when he sent me a picture of him and his son. There was always some excuse. I should have known something was up when he lied about his birth year. Who in the hell lies about their birth year?

This is the day I took back what I was giving away for free: me, my heart, my love, my time, my emotions, and my energy. I took it all back from someone who turned out to be a manipulator, user, abuser, and taker. Someone who opened my love box and toyed with my emotions. This was the day I recognized that I was a side piece, an anytime piece, a part-time lover, and a mistress at the same time.

All the years of putting myself back together were shattered in a ten-minute conversation. From my self-esteem to my physical body, I worked hard to pull myself out of the deep depression that my ex left me in. On the outside, I looked fine, but on the inside, I was fighting to stay afloat. Trying to take care of myself and three other personalities is enough to drive me batshit crazy.

Since I was the only provider for my kids at this time, I experienced tremendous pressure to ensure they got what they needed for everyday living. Their personalities were so freaking different. Keeping up with their emotional rollercoasters was even more difficult because I had a difficult time dealing with my own issues. I was raised during the time of *put your big girl panties on and suck it up.* It wasn't working. My lack of confidence, long-running insecurities, fear of success, being left alone, and lingering in an unhealthy relationship paralyzed my ability to move forward. This is the day I began writing my feelings out.

Here I was, a 40-something-year-old single mom of three children with no one to call my own. Months have passed since this unfortunate event in my life. I had to reinvent myself from top to bottom—the way I thought about things, the way I spoke, the way I moved. I had to reprogram my life as I knew it. One day, I met someone out of the blue. Let's call him Mr. Dimples. He had the prettiest smile and the kindest voice. He was polite and genuine. At the time I met Mr. Dimples, I was busy working on myself. To tell you the truth, I really wasn't looking to start anything because I was still healing.

Only God knows the plans he has for us. This man was stuck in my head as I tried my best to stay focused on my self-healing, but something was drawing me to him. Our chemistry was powerful. His conversation was easy, and right then and there, I said to myself: *He is my significant other.* He treated me with respect and pushed me to be the best version of myself. I was spoken to with respect and allowed to express my needs and wants. And he complied. This was new territory for me. I didn't know how to act. I was always thinking there was a catch-22, but it turns out I got a good one.

Mr. Dimples was teaching me lessons I'd never learned before—**what it meant to be in a healthy relationship.** Words of encouragement spilled from his mouth regularly while catering to my physical and emotional needs. This is important. Listen carefully. When a man takes his time to ensure that you're taken care of in the bedroom and says things like, "I am pleased when you react to me," it's a mind-blowing experience. It takes some time to get used to. For years, I've programmed myself to believe that pleasure was only just for the man. My job was to ensure he was satisfied with what I had served him in the bedroom. So, to have someone put me first was life-altering.

Shared goals and aspirations. It was refreshing to have an intelligent conversation about the future and what the plan was to get there. I never had those types of conversations. It was always about what they wanted to do and how they were going to get there, never how we were going to get there.

Quality time. This was a big one for me since my love language is Quality Time, according to *The Five Love Languages by Dr. John Gray.* Being able to understand the work grind and all it encompasses plays a major part in understanding not all free time is "us time." For example, not all of his downtime was meant for me. I felt if I wasn't in front of him all the time, then he was doing things with someone else. He encouraged me to search for something to do with my time. My day should be filled with my goals and ambitions. I could begin visualizing what it was I wanted out of this life. So, when there was time for us to link up, it was sweet and well deserved. Conversations about the gains made on both our ends were lively, filled with enthusiasm, and productive. This made the time we did have with each other well worth the wait. Time spent together without anger, regrets, or arguments were just blissful moments. When we had them, we were both in the moment.

Communication. I made it a point to always express my feelings, likes, dislikes, and concerns. To have someone listen and take notes and express themselves in turn, in a caring voice, was refreshing. He encouraged the conversation and offered suggestions. He also mentioned dislikes at the same time, not in a harsh or demanding voice but in a "Hey, I got something to say, too" way.

Trust and Honesty. Knowing he was doing the same thing, keeping himself just for me—making a commitment. Seeing someone or being with someone outside of the relationship is unacceptable behavior, and I knew that he would not receive that. The excuse of being lonely is no longer an acceptable excuse for giving my body to someone else. In his mind, I was never his from the beginning. It stands to reason that we're not in a monogamous, committed relationship if I was still willing to have sex with someone else. I knew from his past experiences that that was a deal-breaker.

Intimacy. I believed intimacy meant sex and a lot of it. I soon discovered intimacy at a whole different level. The first time we watched a movie together, we were comfortable and natural with each other, talking, cuddling, drinking, and laughing, and we fell asleep. I woke up first. Instead of feeling happy and relaxed, my brain was scrambled due to memories of other mornings just like this one. I was scared. I was thinking: *Oh no, I didn't give him any pussy. Is he upset? Maybe I can get a quickie before he leaves.* That didn't happen. He had to go to work. By this time, I'm a nervous wreck. I hesitated to ask, but I had to know. "Hey honey, are you okay? I realize you didn't get your *little sum sum* last night or this morning." He laughed out loud, which cheered me up. "I had a wonderful time as always. I look forward to the next time." Say what? That was the moment I fell in love. The thought, *He just wants sex from me all the time,* washed away. The thought, *He actually enjoys me,* was its replacement. That feeling of being wanted and not feeling used lifted from my soul. I found someone interested in *me,* all of me, the real deal me, and it felt good to be recognized as more than just a toy, a pussy, or an ass. This was a turning point in our relationship. I don't know if he knew that, but it was for me at least.

Confidence. Statements of "You're ready" and "You got this" flowed from his mouth regularly. When I first heard this, I was thinking, *Why is he blowing smoke up my ass?* But I soon realized he was being supportive. The more I heard it, the more my confidence increased, not in an "I'm that boss lady" way but damn near close. The boost was refreshing. Paying it forward, making sure he felt my support, and boosting his confidence, in the same way, indicated my appreciation. I also encouraged him to pursue his goals, dreams, and aspirations and later praised him for his accomplishments.

To ensure I was moving in the right direction of healing, I had to build a strong foundation with key elements from life. The powerhouse behind these key elements is through my practice. I must practice them religiously until they become a part of who I am. I must become my priority while on this journey of self-discovery. I realize the road is not going to be easy, and it's going to take a while however, I know the self-work is worth it. Here are some of the practices that I instituted to guide me.

THE PRACTICE

Part One: This is a writing exercise, so get your journal out.

- What does a healthy relationship look like to you? Write down your top five.
- Do you have a healthy circle? Who are you giving your time, effort, and energy to? Are they supportive?
- Write down how you will achieve your goals in the following categories: **Relationships, Health, Finances,** and **Personal Development.**

Part Two: Self-Care

- **Change your Negatives into Positives:** The instant you begin to think the old (negative) way, stop yourself and turn it into a positive thought.
- **Listen to an Affirmation Meditation Soundtrack:** Every morning, have your cellphone programmed to a soundtrack of choice. Here are some suggestions: *"I AM"* by Beautiful Chorus, *"I AM Enough"* by Beautiful Chorus, and *"I AM Everything"* by Beautiful Chorus.

- **Be Kind to Yourself:** Life happens. Give yourself a break. Be your priority, and all will fall into place.

- **Be Your First Priority:** You come first. Your focus should be on you before anyone else—set boundaries. Think along the lines of if they don't add to your life, they aren't a priority.

- **Find an Activity That Brings You Peace:** Carve out time for this activity. Place it in your calendar, and don't allow anything or anyone to detour you from that activity. This is your *"you* time."

Tanya Stokes is a Washington, DC, native by way of the suburban life in Lanham, Maryland. She is a member of Sigma Gamma Rho Sorority, Incorporated, and her local Life Journeys Writers Guild in Waldorf, Maryland. In 2018, she took a leap of faith and founded Compassionate Designs LLC, a graphic design company. She embodies the meaning of the word compassionate (feeling concern for others) in every project she undertakes. She invests her time and energy into understanding her customers, embeds their essence into the project, brings their thoughts into reality, and most importantly, alleviates the burden of navigating how to visualize their brand.

Soon after founding Compassionate Designs LLC, Tanya again answered the call of her entrepreneurial spirit, founding Compassionate Designs Publishing, a publishing company. This venture began with inspiration from a close friend and author who sought to help other authors achieve their dreams of publishing their work without the exorbitant costs associated tithe well-connected publishing companies. Compassionate Designs Publishing aims to assist aspiring authors with publishing services that fit their budgets.

Connect with Tanya:

Website: https://www.compassionate-designs.com

Website: https://www.deskoftanya.com

Amazon: https://www.amazon.com/author/tanya.stokes

Email: compassionatedesigns.llc@gmail.com

CHAPTER 10

THE BALANCED UNICORN

MANAGING OVERWHELM WITH EASE

Denise M. Smith

MY STORY

I thought I was in the clear. I thought this baby would make it.

On April 18, 2002, I went in for what I thought was a quick visit to my obstetrician to check in on our baby. But unfortunately, the baby was now 13 days past the due date. Dr. Sermons smirked at me and told me to go straight to the hospital because we were having a baby *today.*

I had my first child at 26. He was born two weeks late and not according to my birth plan. He was breech, and after Dr. Sermons put his entire right hand and forearm up in my vagina to turn the baby, I had to have an emergency C-section.

"It's a boy!"

"A boy!" I squealed, and at that moment, the numbing sensation of my limbs softened. *I grew an entire penis inside of me!* I was shivering and shaking uncontrollably, which is often a side effect of an epidural. I desperately wanted to hold my son, but the nurses insisted I wait until he was all checked out. My birth plan prudently stated that I'd nurse my baby upon arrival and have plenty of skin-to-skin time. Instead, the nurses forced a different method. Maybe it was because I was a young mom, or perhaps because I was a woman of color, structural racism coupled with implicit biases was in full effect. Whatever it was, I felt like I was talking to myself. Their communication felt like stern commands you'd say to a pet when they had a potty accident. Little did I know that this birth experience would set a precedent for my life 14 years later.

I grew up in a town where my family and three others were the only people of color. By people of color, I mean biracial, Asian, and African-American. I spent all my school years being one of two in a classroom full of non-people of color, which taught me the true meaning of perseverance and being authentic.

When I married Wesley in September 2012, we immediately went into family planning. I was 36, and Wesley was 40. We were determined to have two more children. What I didn't know was that my body had another plan. So, we started our fertility journey, and after three miscarriages and what felt like Groundhog Day in my first trimester and two dilations and curettage (D&C) procedures, we gave up. No more. I was done. Wesley was done. So, we decided to adopt a dog.

I'm a black woman in a world with some doctors who know nothing about black maternal health, which produces disastrous outcomes. I witnessed the birth of a baby that was 25 weeks gestation. I observed dismissive behavior towards the mother, one of my best friends. Because of this, I wasn't excited. I also didn't want to re-fantasize what it would be like to have children with the man I married. I didn't want to die.

"You're pregnant" are the words I will never forget. It was three days before Father's Day weekend (June 2015). It was four months since my last miscarriage, and I wasn't feeling well. I had a terrible headache and was nauseated. Out of the process of elimination, the nurse took a pregnancy test. My heart burst for a moment, and I felt a tingling rush in my abdomen. I was dumbfounded. Did we create a tiny seed all by ourselves? No hormone injections and no providing semen specimens? I was shocked, excited, and scared. "Babe, I'm pregnant." "Okay. Great. Are you taking the pre-natal stuff?" "Yep!"

We were headed to the beach for the weekend with friends, and in fear that our baby wouldn't be viable, we decided not to tell them. I was around five weeks. This baby was due on February 14, 2016.

I was 24 weeks and had completed another yoga class. I saw my belly move, and it felt like it was repeating my entire yoga flow in utero. I couldn't stop grinning ear-to-ear. Then, I went to the restroom and was immediately frightened when I looked down and saw bright red in the water. Tears began to roll down my face. I ran out of the yoga studio and immediately called my obstetrician, who instructed me to go to the emergency room.

My husband rushed me to the ER, and as the nurses checked me in, I saw a familiar face. Mr. Baker, my friend Ashley's father, was in the waiting room because she was giving birth to her son. For a moment, the world around me stopped. *Breathe.* I started to see stars and sat down to prevent myself from passing out. I was scared. The nurses sporadically entered the room with a stethoscope and blood pressure cuff to check my vitals and a heart rate monitor to observe the baby's heart in utero. They didn't say much nor provide much insight into what was happening.

I kept quiet. My mind was racing, and words weren't forming. I felt invisible. *Can they see me? Are they going to tell me that I should not have been doing yoga, considering I was a high-risk pregnancy?* I didn't want to interrupt them because I didn't want them to confirm I was miscarrying. I started to feel like this was all my fault. I began to fiddle on the phone and check in with work. I hadn't told my boss I was pregnant yet. "Denise! How are you?" "Well, I am in the hospital. I am 24 weeks pregnant, and. . ." she cut me off. "Oh. Wow. I had no idea. Does anyone know? Why didn't you tell us this earlier?" I was taken aback. Her response disturbed my inner peace. *Why would anyone ever shame someone for not telling them they were pregnant sooner?* As quickly as I was on the phone, I was off. I knew it was not on me to share my previous pregnancy trauma with my boss; however, her lack of empathy was shocking as a woman!

I stayed in the hospital for four days while nurse Pookie mothered me. I'm not too fond of needles and have braved several rounds of fertility treatments. When the nurse came to have me sign a consent form giving me antenatal steroid treatments with a tool that looked like a knitting needle, I immediately signed. I wanted nothing but to save the baby. Nurse Pookie made me promise to rest until I hit week 34. She divinely insisted: "The antenatal steroid treatments accelerate the maturation of the baby's lungs, which reduces the likelihood of infant respiratory distress syndrome and infant mortality." I began to feel at peace. No matter the outcome, I knew we did everything possible to save it. Why did I call the baby it?" Because I still wasn't ready to claim the living being in my body. I couldn't bear the feeling of another piece of my heart being ripped out of my chest.

At 34 weeks, I woke feeling damp as if I sat on a patio chair after it rained. My water broke while I was sleeping. I took several deep breaths and remembered what nurse Pookie told me: *"Make it to 34 weeks, and everything will be okay."* I pulled myself out of spiraling into doomsday and whispered to Wesley, "Babe, my water broke!" I proceeded to take a shower. I put on a shirt that hung like a dress. Amniotic fluid was still flowing down my legs when we arrived at the ER. I was soaking wet. I felt like I had no control over my limbs, but I gleamed with joy over the anticipation of holding the baby. After all, this was the same ER I was admitted to ten weeks prior. What else could go wrong?

My obstetrician was not on call that morning, and a celebrity was giving birth in another room nearby; no operating rooms were available. *Are they going to make me wait?* I felt sharp pains like daggers digging into my stomach, which started to intensify.

The doctor asked us, "Would you consider having a vaginal birth?" She felt the baby would be small enough and could be pushed out in the room we were in, regardless of the previous scar tissue from my son's cesarean birth 14 years prior. I remember asking what the complications would be if I tried. Her response immediately overwhelmed us, "Something could rupture, and your baby could drown as it begins to crown." We decided against a vaginal birth, signed paperwork, and were immediately added to the emergency c-section schedule. At that moment, I felt in control and empowered to make decisions for our baby's birth plan.

As a black woman, I didn't want to die or for my baby to die during birth. I became awakened to the reality of these birthing scenarios for women of color. The CDC reported that black women are three times more likely to die from a pregnancy-related cause than white women. Multiple factors contribute to these disparities, such as variation in quality healthcare, underlying chronic conditions, structural racism, and implicit bias.

As the operating nurses prepped me for birth, I had a vasovagal response to the epidural and passed out. Once I awoke, the c-section began. I looked at my husband dressed in a scrub suit, noticing he had nothing on under it but his boxer briefs! Just picturing him putting on the scrub suit made me giggle as the operating doctor tugged my stomach. Finally, the doctor looked up at me sternly and confirmed there was no way I could have had this baby vaginally. She sounded relieved. I started to see dark spots and felt lightheaded. I was anxious. I thought, *no shit Sherlock!*

When I couldn't get ahold of the operating notes from my son's birth 14 years prior, we decided to schedule a c-section. The main reason was the unknown scar tissue. *How could she not know this? Why was a vaginal birth even an option?* When they pulled the baby out, I didn't hear anything. I felt like I couldn't breathe. My hands were sweating. I began to panic. *Is this baby alive? Did we get this far only to be disheartened?* "Please, God let my baby live; I promise to take care of my baby the best way I know how." After a few audible breaths, my baby cried. Wesley cheerfully smiled and blurted out, "It's a girl!"

She was 4 pounds 15 ounces with a head full of straight black hair. All I wanted to do was hold her, but the team of nurses rushed her to the neonatal intensive care unit (NICU). I was shocked because though we decided not to find out about the sex of our child until birth, I knew I was having another boy. A big breath left my lungs as I noticed my daughter's beautiful face. She was tiny but mighty. Our lovely little bag of brown sugar was finally here.

I thank the universe daily for giving us the intuition to say no.

No one prepares parents for what happens when their baby is taken to NICU. I was familiar with the NICU because my goddaughter Dylan was born 25 weeks at the same hospital four years prior. The doctors estimated that Zara would be in the NICU for three to four weeks. They explained that we would likely go home without our baby. Tears flowed down my face as I placed the breast pump on both breasts. I knew she needed me. My nipples felt tender to the touch. As the pump sucked my sore nipples, tiny colostrum drops began to drip. My milk hadn't come in. *Breathe. She is here. She will be okay.* "I want to see my baby, now!"

The nurses wheeled my hospital bed into the NICU. Zara was hooked to many wires band-aided to her chest and tiny abdomen. There were beeping sounds, like a box truck backing up. She had a small red tube coming out of her nose. It was a feeding tube. *Had they given our baby formula?* I felt a rush of heat in my face. *Breathe. She is okay. She will be okay.* Can I nurse her?" "Sure," the nurse replied and set me up to hold Zara skin to skin. She placed Zara on my chest, and I could feel thumping against my skin. My heart raced. She's here. Everything is going to be okay.

I thank the universe daily for giving us the intuition to say no.

"One tool on our self-love journey is being able to say no. No empowers us from becoming less people pleasers so that we can take care of the most important person—ourselves."

~ Stephanie Bailey.

My past miscarriages traumatized me, and there weren't many fertility pre and post-partum support groups for people of color like they have today. I had no one to talk to. No one understood my fears except for Wesley and Dionne (my goddaughter's mother and one of my best friends).

Wellness is something I take for granted. I'm always making sure my immediate family and friends are well, but I manage to forget about restoring my energy. After several miscarriages, I had a baby at 34 weeks gestation, and I never took the time to sit with any of my feelings.

I was laid off from a job just as my family returned to our financial stride. I had many moments of uncertainty that caused ignorance or denial of the strain on my wellbeing. Then, I received yet another email rejection stating that though I wasn't a good fit for the role, they wanted to consider me for another position. Even though there was positivity in that message, I felt defeated.

Who wouldn't? After being terminated at work, my daughter's therapy sessions were cut-off. And it took over five months to get reinstated. And then the inevitable happened, our beloved pup Lazer passed away; I felt like another baby was ripped from my soul.

I was at a pivotal point where I needed a permanent time out or a trip to the psych ward in a straight jacket. My mind and body had nothing left to give. I needed to get away. It was time for me to retreat. So, I unapologetically booked my flight and headed to Nizao, a city in the province of Peravia in the Dominican Republic, to participate in my first wellness retreat.

The morning practice and evening ceremonies were just right. They forced me to return to myself and focus on "Who Am I?" The evening ceremonies were magical. There is something extraordinary when you write out what you're leaving behind and what you're moving forward with. We spent time setting our intentions in one of our last yoga sessions. When we returned to our reality, I pressed my hand to my chest and immediately felt my heart beating like someone dancing to African drums—a feeling I hadn't felt in a long time. Tears instantly flowed down my face when I pressed my head onto my mat to send my intentions into the universe. At that moment, at age 45, I knew I would be okay. I can do big things. I am the goddess of my universe.

I felt incredibly sexy; I swam in the ocean naked and meditated in a hammock as the sun warmed my noni. I stood on the ocean bed and allowed the waves to hit my feet, and soon my ankles sank into the pebbles. Each wave drew me closer and closer to the ocean. I finally surrendered my fears. My shakti energy was awakened and reconnected. I felt ready to reemerge, planting seeds whose fruit would be borne by others.

One of my favorite moments was when one of the women wrote a poem about our five days together.

> *"Six divine sisters, a coven of ocean nymphs. Twinkling stars in the sky's darkest hour. Ripe, juicy titties and pussies with power. Six divine mothers invoke the dark Goddess before the fire. Guided spirit. Plant magic. She burned for her desire. Retreat. Release. Recharge. Reemerge."*
>
> ~ Jessica Ward

Coming back home, I felt like a new woman. I reemerged revitalized, ready to show up as a wife, mother, sister, cousin, and friend the best way I knew. I am grateful to my supportive, understanding husband for allowing me to take this space that reconnected us.

THE PRACTICE

"Life is coming. Just get on top of it and ride it."

- Lauren Shields, Wellness Practitioner
website: https://www.merakimamacollective.com

Being able to get away and sit and process everything that had been going on in my life was necessary for my wellbeing, and as women, we often forget this.

I found peace releasing oppressive fears. They held my tongue from authentically expressing myself. I reclaimed crying, screaming, dancing, and laughing to release my shiva energy. I shared traumatizing experiences uninterrupted by judgmental statements. I would no longer let people try to tell me who I am. "You're too nice." "You're doing too much." I acknowledged that critical commentary from the people I trusted most made me feel like jumping out of a moving vehicle. What I needed was to be spoken to with kindness.

"No new friends," is what I said to myself. Conversely, I met folks with whom I will have a connection for life. Over the years, Lauren and I unintentionally formed a relationship that helped me gain new perspectives on my self-love. She affectionately calls me a butterfly. Attending my first retreat with her as the spiritual guide gave her and me a clearer understanding of the balanced unicorn I am. I saw myself in her eyes which encouraged me to release other folks' projected fears. Those judgmental projections would no longer be allowed in my safe space.

Take time for yourself. Dance to your favorite playlist, grab your favorite beverage, and go for a long walk. Go on a wellness retreat. Whatever you do, take the time to restore and reemerge. You can be a balanced unicorn.

Denise Smith is currently the chief technology officer at Newhouse Project Consulting. She is also a micro-influencer as a chief empathy officer at #BiasCorrect. She is known in her community as a globally connected philanthropist and investor who is determined to build a better working world for the next generation. She believes in investing in experiences for youth to provide them exposure that will impact their future trajectory.

Denise began her wellness side gig in March 2018 when she became a barre above certified trainer. She graduated from Spelman College with a bachelor of science degree in May 1999 and obtained a master of business administration from the Georgia Institute of Technology in December 2014. Having a weekday career in the corporate world, group fitness is where her passion for health and wellness can be set free. For over 15 years, yoga, barre, kickboxing, and spinning have facilitated her to elevate her physical, mental, and spiritual wellbeing.

Denise has run/walked 10Ks, is a passionate conference speaker and moderator, participated in team races (Rogue Runner), trained for a triathlon, snowboards, and paddleboards, lived in India, worked with 152 countries, and is an avid bike ride around the city lover. She is a wife (Wesley – Morehouse College c/o 1994), mom of three (Kevin - Morehouse College c/o 2024); (Zara - age 6), fur baby (Lazer the labradoodle – age 12), proud auntie (BJ, Ayla, Brooklyn, and London), sister (middle child – Matrice and Ben), daughter (James and Mary) and daughter in law (Joe, Laura, and Harriette). She grew up in Connecticut, but Georgia is now her home. You can usually find her hanging out with family and friends, preferably outdoors with music, sand, and a body of water.

Connect with Denise:

Website: https://www.denisensmith.com

LinkedIn: https://www.linkedin.com/in/denise-smith-she-her-hers-70ba6a3/

Website: https://www.mostvaluablekids.org/atlanta

Website: https://www.passportatlanta.com

Website: https://www.everygirlshines.org

CHAPTER 11

SURVIVING A DIFFICULT DIVORCE THEN MARRYING A YOUNGER MAN

HOW I FOUND THE LOVE OF MY LIFE IN THE PROCESS—ME!

Christine Falcon-Daigle, MFA, RYT-200

MY STORY

After I signed my divorce papers—ending my 14-year marriage, I exited the courtroom alone. I could hear my ex and his team of lawyers congratulating each other behind me. Thanks to the Xanax my doctor prescribed, I maintained my composure—barely. *Chin up, don't look back.* I felt numb as I walked, carefully balancing on my high heels. My footsteps echoing on the terrazzo floor seemed to belong to someone else.

It was a scorching summer day. When I got to my car, the dam broke. Sobs racked my body like sets of waves in a violent storm. I alternately blew my nose and wailed until the heat inside the car forced me to open the windows. I sat forward in the driver's seat and peeled my sweat-soaked blouse off my back to get some airflow going. I checked the mirror—my face was covered with black streaks from my mascara; my eyes were puffy and swollen.

I married my first love right after college. Despite promising that we'd never get divorced, we officially ended our 20-year relationship in June 2012. The decision was mutual but arriving at it involved a long, painful journey that spanned many years.

A year earlier, when we first appeared in court to file the initial papers, we told the judge our wish was not to involve lawyers. Ours was such an open-and-shut case, a family law mediator present in the courtroom that day followed us out into the hallway and offered to take our case. She said, "You guys will be easy," and that she'd help us draft our Marital Settlement Agreement. We looked at each other and let out a huge sigh of relief.

We worked together for a few weeks, and just before the goal line, things took a dramatic turn.

I grew anxious and fearful of signing the settlement, even though it was very favorable to me; he became frustrated that I wouldn't sign it. Some hurtful things were said by both of us and, out of spite, I refused any amount of alimony.

"In more than 20 years of practicing family law, I have never seen such a bizarre about-face," our mediator said to me later on the phone.

In retrospect, I can see how afraid we both were, scarred from the horror stories we'd heard growing up amidst a culture of divorce—one that said men get screwed in divorce; the other, women. The movie Kramer vs. Kramer was popular when we were kids, and the irony of it all: we both came from divorced families.

Things deteriorated quickly after that, becoming more complicated and contentious, then downright adversarial. It brought out the worst in us both. As if that wasn't painful enough, he sued for full custody of our daughter, alleging I was an unfit parent and that the new home I found for us was unsuitable.

I was so naïve when it came to these matters and didn't even know what a court order was. My lawyer called me the morning I was supposed to be at the courthouse and said, "If you don't get here by the time court starts, he wins." Just out of the shower, I said, "Wins what?" I was half-dressed, focused on getting myself and my eight-year-old out the door on time for school and work. "The court will award him full custody of your daughter!"

The shock waves of ten thousand atomic bombs hit my body with full force at that moment. I dropped the phone, threw my stuff in my car, and sped the whole way, running from the car to the courtroom to my seat beside my lawyer just as the gavel came down, signaling court was in session. Nearly hysterical, I was convinced the packed courtroom could hear my heart pounding as the clerk said, "All rise," and the judge in his black robe took the bench.

The next few months were a blur.

We were required to meet with a court-appointed mediator, someone accustomed to dealing with custody battles in high-conflict divorces. I submitted letters of support on my behalf written by other parents, our daughter's teacher, and my boss. Even though I knew it was his attempt to make his own life easier by moving our daughter to a different county and school system, part of me wondered if I really *was* a terrible mother. His allegations plagued me with self-doubt. *Maybe our daughter is better off without me?*

The whole thing was a mess. I cried every single day. I lost my appetite and could barely sleep. My hair fell out in clumps, and when I went to the doctor, I found out I was severely anemic. At a certain point, I nearly gave up and gave in from the overwhelming stress of it all. But, in the end, we were awarded 50/50 custody, all I'd wanted from the beginning.

During all this, I was romantically involved with a younger man named Jake. He'd moved out to California on the heels of Hurricane Katrina, and he was introduced to our family by our contractor, a mutual friend renovating our house. In the beginning, we were all friends, and he fit right into the fold.

From day one, Jake took my breath away. When I looked into his eyes for the first time, I traveled in a flash across the galaxy without leaving my kitchen. Our souls instantly recognized the other. I heard myself say, "You're cute." It made us both blush. Whenever he was near, my entire body trembled. My stomach filled with butterflies. Within minutes, an involuntary heat spread out between my legs, and my underwear would be soaked. *This is ridiculous; I'm a grown woman, a wife, and a mother!*

I tried hard to deny my feelings at first, then realized it was futile. Once I admitted my feelings of desire to myself, I knew I had to tell my husband. Before anything sexual between us started, he was fully aware of the situation and consented in hopes that it might rekindle the dying embers of our passion.

Jake was someone I thought would never work out in the long run. He was too handsome, too sexy, too young, and way too much fun. Besides, I had all this baggage, and it was complicated. Certain he'd leave, I figured it was just a matter of time.

We both loved the sea and spent a lot of time at the beach, picking up sand dollars and sea glass. We took long drives in complete silence. He wrote poetry and studied Japanese. He had beautiful hands with long fingers that loved to garden, cook, play music, draw, and make things. He was the most comforting and comfortable presence I'd ever known. I was falling in love but wouldn't allow myself to admit it. I didn't know if I'd ever get married again, but for the time being, he was a great companion and lover who gradually became my best friend.

He stood by me as all the fallout from my first marriage rained down. Despite our 13-year age difference, our connection was magnetic. We were nearly inseparable. We'd shared space so effortlessly in a rental by the sea that, when my nesting arrangement collapsed, and I had to find a new home for my daughter and me, he came with us.

The two had grown close by then, sharing lots of silly laughs and inside jokes. Anyone could see the bond they shared was truly extra-special and so clearly what we all needed at that time; I didn't have the heart to end it. And why should I? A vision of a new family began to emerge at this time: me, Jake, and our daughter. It felt so easy and familiar.

During this time, my best male friend—who was like an older brother/ guardian angel—was diagnosed with a rare form of cancer in his foot. I spent as much time with him as I could, squeezing in visits on breaks from work or by giving him a ride to his appointments in San Francisco, where I was attending grad school. I graduated in 2012, the same year I finalized my divorce, and less than a year later, he was gone.

The shock and grief of it, on top of the collapse of my first marriage, and the stress of working nearly non-stop, was too much.

"Let's go somewhere, just the two of us," I suggested, and Jake agreed. We barely had the money to fly to Cabo San Lucas and couldn't get away for more than a few days, but we scraped enough together for airfare, then drove to Todos Santos, *El Pueblo Magico*—the Magic Town.

It was here on a massage table that I had a vision of my friend who'd died. He came to me and said, "If Jake asks you to marry him, say yes!" Uncertain about the idea, I questioned this message and even argued with his spirit. Eventually, he convinced me by giving me an unquestionable sign.

Soon after we returned from Mexico, Jake did propose in his typically understated way by saying we should exchange rings in a ceremony. It took me a few days to realize what he'd said.

"Are you saying we should get married?" I asked.

He nodded. "Yeah, that's what I said." Then we both laughed at my oversight. He said, "I was wondering why you didn't say anything!"

I felt like a giddy schoolgirl, and delight rushed up and out of me, but I was still hesitant. I struggled with daily waves of fear and anxiety back then. All the *what-ifs* and stories about Jake being *too good to be true*. I feared the bottom would drop out any second, hypervigilant about any other woman I caught him looking at. I compared myself relentlessly to others, an exhausting and nearly crippling habit I've had to work hard to overcome.

Later that week was Valentine's Day, and we shared our news with our families, including our daughter, whom we took with us on a fancy dinner date. When we told her we'd decided to marry, we all shared tears of joy and laughter.

Before I could wholeheartedly say "yes" to marrying Jake, though, there was something important I needed to do.

I took myself to a remote beach where I hiked through a field of cows and was followed, amazingly enough, by a falcon—my spirit animal. When I reached the bluffs overlooking the mighty Pacific, I stood at the edge of the continent, where the land ended and the ocean began. I removed my wedding band, the one engraved with my first husband's initials, our wedding date, and blessed by the Catholic priest who officiated our fairytale wedding, complete with horse-drawn carriage and dove release.

I drew my hand back and threw the ring as far as I could into the crashing waves below. Gathering all my strength, I yelled into the wind, "I take myself back!" as I watched the symbol of my first misguided but well-intentioned attempt at marriage disappear into the churning sea foam. The falcon circled overhead and, to my astonishment, let out a shrill cry.

"Today, I marry myself!" I cried, placing my hands on my heart. "I will never give myself away again!" Salty tears ran down my face into my mouth as the sun warmed my back and the waves rolled in, one set after another. When it was time to walk away, I felt it deep inside.

That was a pivotal moment in my life.

Later that summer, on the Fourth of July, my grandparents' wedding anniversary, and a day Jake and I refer to as "Interdependence Day," we exchanged rings and vows, standing in a circle of stones laid out that morning in the green grass, dotted with tiny white flowers.

Our daughter was 11 and stood as my maid of honor. Only our closest immediate family and a few friends were present, surrounded by a grove of tall trees perched above the cerulean waters of the Pacific. We honored the Four Directions and our ancestors, who made themselves known by the sudden wind that rushed through the trees as we tried to light our individual tapers and join them together in a single flame.

Besides our jasmine leis, handmade for us by a native Hawaiian woman in our area, my handsome farmer husband grew all the flowers for our wedding, even my bridal bouquet: sunflowers, dahlias, zinnias, coreopsis, and penstemon. They were stunning! Our wedding day was the most amazing, dream-come-true—not the childish Disney version with a handsome prince who'd rescue me, but the one I'd always longed for: my *anam cara*—soul-mate—standing amongst the trees, under a wide-open sky with nothing but love between us. The memory of it still brings me to tears.

Our wedding night was even more of a dream. My first wedding ceremony was all for show. We were both so tired at the end of it that we didn't even consummate the marriage. This time, it was a whole new experience.

We had decided to practice celibacy for a month or so before our ceremony, giving ourselves the added pleasure of that additional build-up.

We also chose not to be intoxicated by anything but love, and both of us were fully present—heart, body, and soul.

The candlelit room was filled with flowers and special gifts. We undressed each other and took our time. I felt all the feelings of a new bride, including an unexpected innocence and certainty that, for the rest of my life, I would be devoted exclusively to loving and being loved by this man—this man who chose all of me, from every imperfection to every magnificent curve. I felt completely seen and loved for the first time in my life, and it was exhilarating to be so intimate with another!

My fear of repeating the past almost sabotaged everything the night before the wedding. I was so nervous and still so traumatized by the fallout from the first marriage; however, I had enough tools and resources at that point to talk some sense into myself. The conversation started before the sun came up and went something like this:

You can't trust him. This is crazy. He'll never be happy with you. As soon as you start aging, he'll leave you. Or decide he does want to father children of his own, only you'll be too old by then. Don't do it, Christine. You're gonna wind up getting hurt again.

The voice tormented me. I sat, catatonic, listening to it go round and round in my head, like a snarl of angry cats, feuding as the sun rose. I almost believed the story it was telling me and called the whole thing off. Then my spiritual self took over.

This was the authentic part of me I'd met and fallen in love with at my Hoffman Process, back when I was still married to my first husband. That essential self I'd reclaimed, and my love of her, had been growing and deepening since then. She was now big enough and capable enough to take the wheel, so to speak. I watched her in my mind's eye step forward on my wedding day, turn to face the scared little girl on the couch, and order her to sit down and shut up!

I needed her strong voice of authority at that moment. I needed to know she could take control and that she had my back. There was a tiny part of me that resisted. *But how do I know I can trust him?*

She unfurled her enormous white wings of light, put a firm but loving hand on my back, directly behind my heart, and said: *You can trust me, Christine.*

I've come to realize she is me, and *I am her,* and she wants me to be happy and have everything I desire—no matter what that looks like to anyone else. I deserve to be happy, to live the life I love, and love the life I live—and *so do you!*

THE PRACTICE

RITUAL

Plan a ritual to honor the end of your marriage. The October after my divorce was finalized, I participated in a *Dia De Los Muertos* procession, a powerful experience that allowed me to mourn and cut ties with the past.

SUPPORT

If you are going through a separation and divorce, find a support group or a good therapist who can help you navigate this major transition in your life, especially if you are also a parent of young children.

COMMUNITY

Get yourself out of the house and out of your head. Create community. For me, work relationships provided a sense of community. So can volunteering, enrolling in a class, or joining a club.

GRATITUDE

Keep a daily gratitude journal. Because I stepped away from a very comfortable life and had nothing to fall back on but myself, I had to rebuild from the ground up.

Focus on simple things: flowers blooming outside the door; the unconditional love of a pet; an extra hour of sleep. Gratitude also attracts more of what we are grateful for!

TRUST

Another way of saying this is: *Fake it 'til you make it.* Write positive affirmations on sticky notes and put them in a place you'll see them every day. Make up silly songs you can sing when you feel scared. Mine is called *"Believe in Yourself,"* and I still sing it to this very day.

DEEPING INTIMACY

Being married to a younger man has been a huge exercise in receiving. I've had to learn how to keep opening my heart to accept this man's love for me.

Set a timer for five minutes. Put a hand on each other's heart and gaze into each other's eyes, a powerful way to give and receive love. You may find this impossible in the beginning. Work up to it.

Breathwork has also helped exponentially by allowing me to feel the power of love from the inside out and with my husband. Find a qualified practitioner and give it a shot!

Christine Falcon-Daigle is an award-winning writer, teacher, and facilitator who's worked in retreat settings dedicated to transformation and consciousness for more than a decade. In 2020, she began shifting her focus to the reclamation of the Divine Feminine, becoming a certified circle facilitator in 2021 with Global Sisterhood. She currently offers monthly in-person sisterhood circles in Marin County, California, and co-facilitates weekly writing circles, online.

Her poetry and fiction have appeared in print, online, and on the stage; she has worked in radio and film, serving as associate producer for The Last Stand (1998), an award-winning documentary that aired nationally on public television and internationally at film festivals. She reads her work regularly at literary events around the San Francisco Bay Area.

In 2012, she completed a two-year program with the Horticultural Therapy Institute (HTI) and, along with her husband, has designed and installed labyrinths, beehives, flower gardens, and food forests. They are currently seeking a property of their own to create a healing sanctuary.

She's a certified blind ski guide and yoga instructor who's taught skiing, yoga, and mindfulness to teens and adults since 1993. She loves to travel and has assisted with international yoga and meditation retreats in Cambodia, Thailand, Haiti, and Mexico.

Along with her love of creative expression and all things wild, she's a self-proclaimed bibliophile who counts libraries and bookstores among her favorite places on Earth.

Connect with Christine:

Website: www.christinefalcondaigle.com

LinkedIn: Christine Falcon-Daigle

Instagram: @cfalconmoon and @transformanity

Email: cfalcone1021@gmail.com

Links/Resources: www.hoffmaninstitute.org

www.globalsisterhood.org

CHAPTER 12

NAVIGATING THE LOSS OF A LIVING CHILD

THE HEALING POSSIBILITIES IN A SPIRITUAL RELATIONSHIP

Marion Noone

MY STORY

I finally got it. The evidence I had been asking for. It came in the form of a picture, and in this portrait laid my husband and a stripper naked in my bed with my newborn baby.

I couldn't breathe. The walls moved towards me. My peripheral vision closed in with black clouds. My tender heart pumped hard and slow. It was all I could hear and feel. My body gave out. My spirit left me. I descended to the floor, landing on my knees, eventually recognizing myself in a fetal position. I cried long, deep sobs for my daddy, who was three hundred miles away. I don't remember much at that moment other than excruciating heartache and my babies seeming really concerned, petting me. I wanted to die. I didn't think I could get up and move on.

Someone, please come kill me. I thought to myself. *This pain is too unbearable.*

"Go upstairs and get the suitcase out of your brother's closet," I asked my oldest daughter.

She was confused but could read something was undeniably wrong. She listened without argument.

I packed the bag and my kids and left. I had 35 dollars, no job, and no income. He controlled all the finances and immediately cut me off when I knew the truth.

Before I go on, I desire to create a safe space for you. I wish I could spend hours with you, face to face, sipping fresh-brewed iced tea dripped with lemon handpicked from the backyard—you and I share our stories, processing them out, crying, releasing together like family, the real kind.

Reading this, I desire for you to envision us together in this safe space. Feel my heart. Feel that family in me and know whoever you are or wherever you are, I love you, and I've got you.

I'm a woman, just like you, colored with trauma and life experience. My battle scars are the same as yours. The road map may tell a different story, but our tears are just as equally wet and salty. You're safe here with me.

So now that you know the space I'm holding for you let's go back to that day. The day my world changed forever.

We were all weeping in my now unaffordable SUV. I didn't even know how to soothe myself, much less four other souls that were just as confused and sad. Heart coherence between a mother and child is a very real experience. Vibrations of their pain rushed through my heart and body like bleeding waves. I couldn't even speak. The cries were so loud. Inner desires to scream begged to be unleashed, but that wouldn't have helped the situation. So, I did what I always do and mentally went to my treehouse. I had to clear the noise and take care of myself.

When I was a little girl, I grew up in a single-parent, abusive, unsafe home where drugs moved in and out. I was raped and molested on many occasions. The floors and walls reeked of dog shit, and piss and roaches became normality for me. When I was scared, I'd hide in the treehouse my daddy built for us on the back of the property before he left. It was my sanctuary.

I'll never forget my first rape.

Close your eyes! I know it hurts, but it's temporary. You've been through a lot. You can overcome this. Just stay quiet. It will be over with soon.

These are the words my seven-year-old self whispered to me when my rapist from down the street was shoving ice inside me. The pain between my legs hurts to this day to revisit. Standing up straight was nearly impossible. I walked from my home barefoot through my yard. I remember it was unseasonably cold. The blood and tears moved from me, creating cool trails that brought an extra kind of chill to my worn body. I had never felt the grass so viscerally nor had so much gratitude for the earth holding me. I had no one to turn to—my soul on the verge of collapse in equivalence to my body. I was almost emotionless; the pain was so severe. Revolving stabbing pains tortured my lower abdomen. Each step up to the treehouse brought just a bit more ease and comfort, enough to keep me motivated to make it up there to rest in peace.

After that day, I developed a personal practice. Anytime I experience a life-altering trauma, I close my eyes and imagine myself in that childhood sanctuary—my treehouse.

So, there I was, driving to a practical stranger's home with four kids, no money, and no idea of my future. Then God (Source) spoke to me. *Tell them about your sanctuary. Tell them about your treehouse.*

"Hey babies, take some deep breaths. Mama wants to talk to you about something special, okay?"

It took a bit to calm four kids. If you're a mom of multiples, you understand. Once all breaths were calm, I said, "I know this is scary, and things will be strange and different for us for a while, but I want you to know when Mommy gets a house, the first thing I'll do before I unpack a single box is build you a treehouse."

Their entire moods changed. Their faces lit like stars on a dark night. We talked about the design, what baby dolls and Lego men were allowed to visit, and what color the walls and makeshift curtains would be. The moment of terror turned into a dream manifestation for us. The refrigerator in my apartment was covered for the next year with Crayola drawings they had all made of our soon-to-come physical sanctuary. I didn't have the strength to throw one of them away. It was a bit ridiculous, ha-ha, but if you're a mama, you know.

After that day, I fought. It felt like a never-ending divorce—a slow drip of all my resources each day growing weaker in mind, body, and spirit. Multiple mediations took place, and ultimately, in the end, I lost custody after what felt like many battles in a revolving war. Having my children ripped from my soul felt like a complete crucifixion—capture and torture by the enemy, ending with defeat. Four years of figuring life out, building a career from scratch, healing from heartbreak, and part-time single mommy-ing four littles was not for the faint of heart.

I did it. I accomplished it. I acquired ten acres and a beautiful mountainside home on north Lake Travis in Austin, Texas. It had three stories of decks with the perfect sunset lake view. The view, though, didn't even compare to the potential treehouse possibilities. So, guess what I did? I built a treehouse, as promised. I had strangers show up to help me who later became lifelong friends. It was a whole project. It was nothing short of magic. Each day we built, more healing took place for me and everyone involved. It became the sanctuary it was intended to be.

We finished just in time, two days before they were coming to visit me for Christmas. It was their Christmas present. The suspense of the surprise was killing me inside. I couldn't wait to see them witness their power of manifestation.

It was Christmas Eve morning. My roommate Drew, and I were having coffee on the front porch watching the beautiful orange glowing sun rise above the mountain. We were both so excited to experience the joy of the kids and to see their faces light up like they did that day in my SUV. A white unmarked car pulled into the driveway shortly after. "Fuck!" Immediate terror overtook me. PTSD on full blast. I began sweating and shaking in utter terror. I already knew what it was. It was the narcissist serving me yet again, another set of papers. A police officer climbed out of the vehicle, and as he approached, I noticed he was in tears.

He said, "Ma'am somedays my job is so rewarding; other days, I consider quitting. I'm so sorry to do this to you on Christmas Eve."

I couldn't even open it, so I asked my roommate Drew to read it and give me a summary. It was an emergency custody order accusing me of being a child molester, along with many other horrifying accusations that were far from the truth. So again, 22 years later, I found myself on another walk of shame. Again, bleeding and tearful, I walked to the treehouse I had built for them and cried until I fell asleep. They never got to see it.

I made a Facebook post admitting to my surrender. White flag, y'all! I couldn't do it anymore. My heart had been broken so many times. I just didn't understand. Why? How could someone be so evil?

An attorney reached out to me on New Year's Eve and picked my case up pro bono. She made so much progress and disproved all the ridiculous allegations. I finally got some visitation back, although I was still paying more than half of my income in child support. My kids were constantly walking on eggshells, terrified to show me love in fear of being punished by my ex and his current wife. It was like this strange dichotomy for all of us. We wanted each other but couldn't be free in the cage the people with money and power had set for us. Eventually, I broke completely and had to surrender. It was in the best interest of all of us. The ultimate mother's sacrifice. My final crucifixion.

To be honest, this journey is incredibly difficult. There is no instant remedy or book you can read that will miraculously take it all away. Grief is a strange experience, and almost weekly, I have difficult days. Sometimes I wake up suicidal, feeling completely and utterly hopeless. However, I'm still here breathing, taking it day by day. Nurturing my own heart with tools like the tools I share in the practice section below has been my lifeline on difficult days. You are not alone in your suffering, and though I wish I could hold you and take all that pain for you, I'm grateful that at least I'm able to provide a few lifelines to help you keep going.

To this day, I still play with my little darlings. I can hear their laughs when I hike in the woods and notice some of their favorite adventures finds. I sing to them often, remembering their smells and sweet sleeping breaths soothed after a heartfelt lullaby. *Colors of the wind* and *The Little Mermaid* song were their favorite songs. I can sense them playing on the floor in the kitchen when I'm cooking. I celebrate their birthdays and holidays by doing special things like writing letters and putting them in the ocean like a message in a bottle. I always write their current address on the bottles in hopes a diver somewhere finds it and ships it to them. They are with me always, regardless of the physical separation. I recommend using all of these tools, but below I've listed two simple lifelines that you can use for the loss and separation of not only a child but apply it to the loss of any loved one.

The physical aspect of our relationships is only a piece of what we share. So, let's look at some other ways to maintain and nourish our relationships with loved ones when the physical is impossible.

THE PRACTICE

CONNECTION MEDITATION

Turn off your phone and make sure you have no distractions for the next 15 minutes. The environment is up to you. Choose a space where you will feel most comfortable. For some, that's a dark room; for others, it's sitting lakeside on a picnic blanket. Make yourself as comfortable as possible. Use all the pillows and blankets you need. Eye pillows are a plus if you're lying down.

Once you're comfortable, **close your eyes and take ten long, slow, deep inhales followed by big exhales, forcing the breath out at the bottom of the exhale.** After the initial breathwork is completed, come back to your natural breath.

Begin to **imagine your child in front of you.** It's completely okay and normal if heavy emotions start to surface. Anytime emotions show up in meditation, allow them to come and use the breath to get through the intensity. Don't judge it. Just let it flow. When you feel calm, grounded, and centered, move to step five.

Imagine what your child smells like. Take yourself to a memory of that smell. Remember the emotion of that smell and sit with it for a few breaths.

Imagine the texture of your child's skin and hair. Feel yourself caressing his/her face or embracing them with a long hug. Remember the emotion you felt during these embraces. Sit with this feeling for as many breaths as you need.

Begin to envision your child in one of their happiest moments and see that smile. That big, bright, joyous smile. Isn't it beautiful? Tap into that joy you felt in your heart observing this.

If you feel you're fully present with them, try talking to them. You can be creative with this part. Imagine a play date or an adventure, and just have fun in the circumstance you choose.

Once you feel at ease, **allow yourself to slowly come out of the meditation.** Be gentle with yourself and take as much time as you need.

After you've come to, I always suggest going outside and putting your bare feet in the grass to ground back to earth and recharge.

I suggest doing this practice at least three times weekly; however, you can do it as much or as little as you please. The best thing to do always is to just start. Try it on for size. See what it feels like, and know you can reach out to me for help or advice at any time.

LETTERS TO YOUR LOVES—A JOURNAL EXERCISE

Get a notebook. Dedicate it to only these letters. I promise it will be easier to have them all in one place, and as time heals your wounds, you will want to revisit these to look back at not only how far you've come but also reminisce about where you were when you wrote each letter.

Get a quality pen. Pens that are easy to write with, help me significantly when I'm journaling. Nothing annoys me more than not having the perfect pen, so take my advice and get that perfect pen for you. It's worth it!

Now we have all the essential ingredients **let's talk about the environment.** You don't need to be picky about this if it's a place you feel safe and free to flow in your writing without distractions or judgments from others in your surroundings. This is a very sacred, vulnerable practice, so my main concerns are you are comfortable, in a safe space, with the perfect materials.

Now that the materials and environment are set **let's talk about the entries.** I have four children, and I don't force these letters, so the timeline and frequency vary depending on my experiences and when each child comes up in my thoughts in my day-to-day life. I don't want these to feel forced or fake. I write from an organic desire.

Just write. Let the pen sweep the page and allow whatever flows to flow. Don't try to make it sound perfect or even that it's from a parent to child. Be real and raw in these entries. Talk to your child as if he/she is a grown adult after a life full of experience. Describe your emotions. Describe your fear and joy and confusion and feelings of loss. Just be honest and real. Tell them you miss them. I'm a strong believer words are medicine but can also be spells. Be sure to stick to kindness and leave out the ex. They don't need that energy. That's between you and him/her. Just be with your child fully in each entry. Make it like you're talking to one of your best friends.

TIPS FOR CONSISTENCY

I keep the journal in my car, and if I'm going somewhere without my car, I always bring an extra bag with my art supplies, which usually consists of my love letter journal, awesome pens, charcoal, chalk, and emergency paper to draw on. I have left my drawing pad behind before, and it's no fun not having paper when you're in the mood to express yourself.

Marion is a free spirit you will often find frolicking in the woods honoring Gaia (Earth) by building offerings and/or cleaning the local lands she visits on her travels. She is a 200RYT certified yoga instructor with seven years of experience and is also Reiki certified. Marion has accomplished jewel rank as an Ambassador for Plexus Worldwide, assisting many men and women across the country with probiotic therapy and safe, natural weight loss practices. She has seven years of experience coaching female entrepreneurs in growing young online businesses. From private retreats to public speaking, she has assisted in teaching budding entrepreneurs to lead their businesses with love and not with the goal of a sale. This has allowed many men and women in financial distress to achieve financial freedom while working from home. Marion often visits cities and offers time and assistance to the local homeless in the community. She has ten years of volunteer experience in long-term care, hospice, and Alzheimer's units. If you wish to learn more about Marion, please visit any of the links below. She enjoys getting to know her readers and is available to all. She loves people, and you won't regret reaching out.

Contact Marion at:

Facebook: (5) Marion Noone | Facebook

Instagram: @warr10rw0n

Email: swampfairy222@gmail.com

Plexus link- www.plexusworldwide.com/southernyogi

Website- www.swampfairy.com

CHAPTER 13

SOUL DIVING

RECLAIMING YOUR AUTHENTIC SELF

Jill Alman-Bernstein

MY STORY

The shrill ring of the telephone shattered the stillness of the night.

Daughter. Hospital. France. Mugged. Sprained neck. Concussion. I felt a hollowing in my chest. The room began spinning. I sunk into the bed and listened as my daughter relayed what had happened. She was alright despite the trauma and injuries. It would just take time to recover from the concussion.

A call from a child in distress, especially from a foreign country over 3000 miles away, is a parent's worst fear and nightmare. You cannot imagine that scenario when you hold your precious soul in your arms for the first time, or as you watch your child take their first steps, or say their first words, that one day you will get a call and hear the terrible news that will change the course of your child's life and yours.

Imagination and dreams of being a mother are powerful passions. I was eight years old when I first pretended I was a mother and gave birth to my make-believe husband and favorite Monkee's child. That memory is so clear. I can see myself and my friend in her room, writhing on the floor, screaming as we magically pulled our dolls from underneath our skirts. Childhood was such a simpler time. My imagination and dreams were filled with the promise of idyllic motherhood. Not once in those play sessions, as I cared for my newly plopped-out baby doll, did I think of anything but the perfect life.

I was one of the "caught in between" generations, the one where we were told we could have it all. Thank you, feminism. And yet, I grew up with the conditioning to get married and have a family. College, graduate school, career, family. That would be my path.

I approached my late twenties all in, career in full swing. It was my 28th birthday. I thought I'd be married and have two kids by the time I was 30. I wasn't close to being married. And two children by 30 was not happening. My tears of despair soaked the streets of New York. A few years later, still juggling my career and dream, I married a wonderful man and proceeded to embark on my path to fulfill my destiny of motherhood.

That call from my daughter in France was just the beginning of her concussion saga. Years later, after she graduated from college, there would be another call. This time it was 2000 miles and across the country. A skiing accident in Telluride, Colorado. "Were you wearing a helmet?" "Yes," she said, "It fell off though when my head hit the ground. I thought I was okay, so I got up and started down the hill, but I skidded, fell, and smacked my head again." I listened to her endless loop of ski, fell, hit her head, and envisioned a cartoon character. I couldn't imagine a human falling and hitting her head as many times as she described. The ER doctor said, "Rest." Stubborn and determined to continue on her post-graduation road trip, she made it to Moab before visiting the ER again. "Stop traveling and rest," she was instructed. I think she rested for a day or two before she pushed on and then finally realized she needed to just come home. But could she get on a plane and come home? The MRI and CT scans were clear. She jumped on a red-eye flight to Boston. I scooped up my puddle of a daughter and brought her home.

With one child out of college, one in college, and one still in high school, I finally created some time and space for myself. I have always loved to dance. I took lessons from a young age, danced with my college dance company and then with a small modern dance company while in graduate school. Dancing was in my blood. Teaching too. I always thought I'd have my own space and studio to dance, dream, teach, and stay connected to myself. I practiced yoga for years but missed dancing and searched for something that bridged my love of dance and the meditative qualities of yoga and other forms of movement. I found and fell in love with Nia Technique - a sensory-based and intuitive movement practice drawing from the martial, dance, and healing arts, intentionally connecting the body, mind, and spirit. Somehow I manifested the time to take the first level certification. I was excited about my newly acquired skill. I was passionate about practicing and helping other women connect to their bodies and souls through intuitive movement combined with breathwork and Nia. I loved going to the dance studio and guiding others. I was in my element. I was in myself.

At the same time my daughter returned home to recover in her childhood bedroom, shades drawn for weeks on end, another child struggled with anxiety and depression. I had two out of three children in crisis. My time at the studio dwindled and then evaporated. I spiraled into the depths of obligation to my children in need.

My idyllic view of motherhood was certainly challenged before. There were the bumps in the road with school, bullying, disappointments, friendships, learning challenges, and the Individual Education Plan that, by law, needed to be observed but wasn't.

We play many roles—daughters, sisters, girlfriends, wives, to name a few—but the role of mother, particularly mama bear, is the most intense. Never did I imagine when I plopped out that baby doll the skillset, resourcefulness, and resilience I'd need as a mother.

I could always find a solution. My husband and kids knew I could fix anything and everything. They counted on it. I was the consummate mother. Ask anyone. Always there for my children. Always putting them before myself. Always knowing what to do. I was consumed with motherhood, enmeshed in every facet. But when we're talking about traumatic brain injuries and the need for a child to be treated for severe anxiety and depression, well, there went my idyllic life, and "the fixer" in me was defeated. The mama bear too.

There is nothing worse than feeling you can't fix what's wrong, that you're without the necessary resources to help your children. *My soul screamed, aching for my pain to be eased.*

Navigating the concussions was not a short trip. It was filled with multiple calls to hospitals and doctors trying to ascertain the best path. There was physical therapy, cranialsacral therapy, acupuncture, an evaluation with a neuro ophthalmologist, and visual stabilization therapy. Did you know that there was such a thing as a neuro ophthalmologist and that most concussions result in some injury to the way the brain processes what we see? Because of the protocol at the time my daughter was concussed, she was what they now call "de-conditioned," and instead of gradually re-introducing herself to her computer screens, being outside and just taking walks, writing, and other basic functioning, she went from zero to ten and found that simple tasks and things that she was so proficient at were no longer in her grasp. It was terrifying for her and for me to watch. My brilliant and creative daughter was reduced. She became despondent and depressed, and I became despondent and depressed along with her.

Meanwhile, my child struggling with anxiety was flailing. I packed him up. It was a scenic drive. Our anguish palpable, my husband and I chatted nonchalantly as my son watched the trees waving as we drove by. Sending my child into residential treatment was one of the hardest things I had to do as a mother. I held him and hoped with all my heart that he'd come out the other side stronger, more confident, and have the tools he needed to manage his anxiety and depression.

When I look back on that time, I honestly don't know how I made it through. I was so overwhelmed. I took everything on, everyone's pain and suffering, and there was a lot of pain and suffering going on. I remember crying in my therapy appointments. I was so depressed. *I failed as a mother; the one thing I felt called to do, knew I was to do. The one thing I knew I'd have a 100% completion rate on in my life, and I failed.*

The worst part of it all was that I lost myself, the connection to my authentic self. I was overwrought. Blocked. Not being able to plant my feet firmly on the ground was unsettling and disabling. I spiraled down to the depths of depression and self-abandonment. I just wanted the emotional pain to go away. I imagined crashing my car into a tree. But I couldn't do anything like that. I couldn't leave my children.

I don't know how long I swam in the murky waters that unfolded to cavernous depths, my every thought pushing me deeper into my own endless darkness.

Each time I tried to pull myself out, I fell back into the quicksand. I did have my inspirational Facebook page that somehow I kept doing. The posts I chose and wrote encouraged my followers and me to look for the positive in life, the rays of light, the silver linings, and the cup half filled. I tried. I took walks on the beach with my dog. I regularly walked with and confided in a dear friend. I tried to remember to breathe, move my energy, and use my crystals, my tools. All were pieces of the puzzle that made up my lifeline to myself.

That was 2016. It seems like a lifetime ago, yet the journey and challenges continue.

My daughter studied creative writing in college but said she could no longer access her creativity and visualize to create and write the way she did pre-concussions. Her health had become tenuous, like the traumatic brain injury compromised her immune system, too. Her judgment, a bit impulsive, concerned her and us. Her once more-than-competent organizational and executive functioning skills were nonexistent. Mama bear to the rescue. Once a fixer, always a fixer. I embarked on a comprehensive research dive. *What doctors could I reach out to? Where were the proper resources to help me help her?* I'm so good at diving into the content, finding the most obscure of the obscure. I circled back to one of the concussion doctors and was led to the Sports Concussion Clinic at Massachusetts General Hospital. I thought she needed a neuropsych evaluation. They agreed.

As luck or bad luck (depending on how you want to view things) happened, my youngest, in a freak at-home accident in May 2021, banged his head and had a severe concussion. The luck was that after a few initial visits to his primary care physician, I expertly whisked him to the concussion clinic that I found for my daughter. The bad luck was that although he was able to finish his remote college term with accommodations for the injury, it was a terrible downhill journey from there. Recovery initially included physical therapy, visual stabilization, and a new visit to the neuro ophthalmologist. He had been evaluated before. When my daughter had her neuro ophthalmology evaluation, I noticed a brochure in the doctor's office talking about kids being misdiagnosed with attention deficit disorders, and it actually is a condition called Convergence Insufficiency. I made an appointment for my child, who always complained of reading challenges, and bingo, he had, in fact, been misdiagnosed. Again, I felt that I failed as a mother. *How could I not know that he needed an eye evaluation when he was in elementary school?* His reading was not a learning challenge or an attention issue but another condition that could have easily been addressed had I or any of his teachers, or special ed consultants identified it. His vision was always 20/20 when tested, so no one caught it. This would have made school so much easier for him and perhaps less anxiety-inducing.

Failure, failure, failure. The mama bear was defeated. Or that's how I felt. "Don't be so hard on yourself," friends and family said. Somewhere I learned self-judgment and self-criticism. I thought I could've somehow changed the course of events. If I just had the correct information and diagnosis from the start—if I could have prevented the concussion—if I had the right resources for helping my child with anxiety. The list went on. I had to learn to let go of that self-judgment and self-criticism.

My three children are all in their twenties now. They are incredible people, caring, loving, good souls. My daughter and youngest son still suffer from the effects of their concussions. Something else I learned on this journey; underlying mental health affects concussion recovery and contributes to long-term challenges. If you're coming into a concussion with depression and anxiety, it all just gets magnified.

And so I encourage and cheerlead them, and myself, to do the things that help keep the anxiety and depression tamped down for all of us. "Use your tools," I tell my son, showing him EFT and sending him meditative music to help him with positive self-talk and restful sleep. "Do your morning yoga and breathwork practice," I remind my daughter, who actually is a certified yoga teacher and knows exactly what to do but gets caught in her own thinking loop. "There are so many good tools," is my daily refrain. From tapping to setting intentions, from yoga poses to tai chi—any movement to move your energy, from listening to relaxing music to sound baths, from walks in nature to ground you, to positive self-talk and affirmations: "So many tools," I say.

I had to find mine, and my way back to myself, to reconnect to who I am, not as a mother, but as an individual separate from my family, as a woman with gifts to share. "You're a mermaid, so dive!" My social media platform, "I Must Be A Mermaid," a guiding force. The Anais Nin quote, "I must be a mermaid, . . . I have no fear of depths and a great fear of shallow living." riveted me to the idea of not living shallowly but diving deep into myself, into life's challenges and writing about it.

And dive, I did. I began looking for something, and that something was myself. I yearned to know what was down deep in my soul. What was my true essence? What was it that I was here to do besides being a mother?

I began by connecting the dots.

I was a dancer. I started to do Nia again to reconnect with my body. I cultivated a breath and movement practice for myself.

I was a writer. I wrote poetry and songs in my younger days and blogged in my older ones. I started to journal more, reflecting on how I was feeling and what I was experiencing.

I was intuitive, hearing and feeling messages from Spirit. I had a direct line to my angels. I embraced that part and started reading angel, oracle, and tarot cards. I felt a calling and learned to read Akashic Records.

I wanted to help other women who felt like I felt: overwhelmed, stuck, or at a loss for what was next for them. I started offering readings and intuitive guidance to clients, creating a program for women to explore their connection to their intuitive and authentic selves. I call it Soul Diving.

Each dot is a piece of the puzzle of who I am, my core essence. Being a mother is a wonderful part of me, an important hat I wear, but a role that does not solely define who I am.

They say every drop creates a ripple effect.

Here are a few drops you can do every day to help you create that ripple that will help you dive into and connect with your soul: a little movement, a little breathing, and then voicing affirmations.

THE PRACTICE

You can do this by your bed, in front of a mirror, outside in your yard, or wherever you feel most comfortable.

Begin by standing barefoot on the floor or ground. Shake out your whole body for a moment—your head, shoulders, arms, waist, hips, legs. Find a comfortable stance, feet hip-width apart. Now put one of the palms of your hand over your heart, and then place your other hand over the first hand. Drop your chin to your chest, close your eyes, and just breathe. Inhale and exhale, noticing your breath, allowing it to flow in and out gently. Notice how it fills your lungs, chest, and heart, how it fills your belly. Feel the expansion of your breath and energy through your body as you inhale. Exhale, allowing your breath to empty out of every part, every cell of your body. Continue to gently inhale and exhale your breath. Now allow your chin to float up so that you are looking straight ahead. Open your eyes.

Choose an affirmation to say in the morning or anytime you need to call on your inner resilience, positivity, and strength. A suggestion is to write or type each affirmation on a piece of paper, put them in a dish, and then pick one each day.

- I am rooted to the earth. I stand firmly in my power and strength.
- With each breath, I feel nurtured and strong. My breath grounds and uplifts me.
- I stand in my self-empowerment, wisdom, and strength.
- I am strong. I am beautiful. I am powerful. I can do this.
- I am safe being myself.
- I am able to create a space where I can sit quietly and connect to my heart and soul.
- I have the resilience to overcome whatever challenges this day brings.

Please visit https://jillalmanbernstein.com/soul-diving/
for more affirmations and practices.

Jill Alman-Bernstein wears many hats, or as she says, she has a lot of plates in the air.

Besides being the mama bear, fixer, and the mother of three amazing 20-something humans, Jill is a writer, a writer's coach, a freelance editor, and an author. Her soul's calling is as a transformational intuitive teacher and mentor who guides spiritual seekers to uncover and step into their soul's authentic and Divine creative expression through the Akashic Records.

Jill has studied and practiced breathwork, yoga, dance, and intuitive movement. She is an Advanced Certified Akashic Record Soul Realignment Practitioner, holds a White Belt in Nia, and is a Certified Belief Clearing Practitioner.

She is a member of two global energy healing groups, working with healing energy for over a decade, and is a Divine Energy Healing Practitioner working with the angelic realm.

Jill is the creator of the Facebook social media platform I Must Be A Mermaid, focusing on inspiration, empowerment, personal growth, and transformation. In her private Facebook group, The Enlightened Mermaid, she reads angel, oracle, and tarot cards.

Truly a mermaid, Jill lives surrounded by water on the island of Martha's Vineyard. Just being in nature, taking walks on the beach with her cockapoo pup, the amazing Arlo, and spending time with her husband and children, brings her great joy. She loves a good rom-com movie or a great Broadway musical too.

At her core, Jill is a deep sea soul diver, always striving to tune in even more deeply to her intuitive self by breathing in the beauty of each and every day.

Connect with Jill:

Website: jillalmanbernstein.com

Facebook: https://www.facebook.com/soulofamermaid/
           https://www.facebook.com/groups/3417097641652139

Instagram: https://www.instagram.com/theenlightenedmermaid/

LinkedIn: linkedin.com/in/jill-alman-bernstein-40755919

Clubhouse @jillabernstein

CHAPTER 14

COMPLETE GUIDE TO PSYCHOLOGICAL AND SPIRITUAL GROWTH

HOW TO AVOID BEING BROKEN DOWN BY ILLNESSES

Nolwazi Charmaine Nkosi

"Being able to walk pain-free is a blessing. Being able to walk without showing the pain is a skill."

~ Kylie McPherson

MY STORY

"Come on, the pictures are beautiful," my twin sister tenderly and genuinely said. She wasn't lying, the pictures were beautiful, but not my skin. All I could see were the dark scars and unpleasant patches of eczema. My mind was screaming: *Delete, delete. No one wants to see those ugly pictures!* Doctor's appointments became a daily bread and a vocal trend: "Oh no, sorry, I won't make it. I have a doctor's appointment."

"Nolwazi, Nolwazi!" I forcefully opened my puffed and stinging eyes. "O-M-G! Are you gonna be able to go to school?" My sister looked at me with teary eyes. "Please call Dad and tell him I need to see the doctor. I'm not well," I finally said to my twin sister after the exams. She knew I wasn't well but didn't think about what I was hiding underneath the long scratchy polar neck T-shirts and baggy pants.

I waited for her to leave, then slowly dragged myself out of the heavy sheets and blankets. I crossed my hands around my chest as I rose, so I couldn't scratch my swollen red boobs. I'd have to do it very softly to avoid peeling off the thin layer of skin.

My scratches were never gentle; I never cut my nails; they were my scratch weapons. My linen had to be washed every two days; they were bloody and covered in damaged, dry skin. Nighttime was the worst; you'd swear the allergy tablets were bouncing off my system with no effect. They were so ineffective that the doctor put me on new routines now and then. I'd wake up with bloody hands and newly developed rash patches. Believe me when I say "the itch-scratch" is real.

Nobody knew I hadn't bathed the previous day; I had a whole outfit of weeping eczema on underneath my PJs.

"Could you please run me a bath?"

"Run you a bath?" My sister wore this concerned look.

I went to the bathroom, slowly hulled off the clothes from my skin, took a deep breath, and sighed. Some places were better than others, and the only normal skin left was the size of my palm and was on my chest. I washed my face; surprisingly, the hot water stung my eyes. That was new, and I didn't want to feel that ever again.

My grandmother could definitely tell that the eczema was the cause of my sudden isolation. I was caught between: *Do I show her and stress her out? Or do I call my dad to come home?* My red face gave signals to my lips—they felt heavier by the second, the margin getting bigger and bigger. My body crawled at the thought of what would happen to the rest of my dried-up and scaly skin. I cried. I sat in the bathroom for almost 20 minutes in tears. After that, I got up, changed, and went to sleep.

"I was told you're sick," my father said as he walked in.

I still hadn't showered, and my mind couldn't bear the thought of coming into contact with water, considering the scales falling off my jersey.

"It's the eczema, nothing major." I became so content with the flare-ups that I didn't want my family to know how much it bothered me.

"Get ready. I'll take you to the doctor."

"Well, I am ready. I can't shower. I just brushed my teeth."

I had no idea what was going on in my father's mind at that time. But I know my grandmother was alarmed the moment she realized I wasn't at school. She somehow knew it was the eczema that made me skip.

"Is the skin bothering you again?" she asked in a low and soft pitch.

"Yes, but I don't think it's that major." I knew my grandma knew it was bad, but I couldn't bear to see her worried, so I forcefully smiled before I left.

"I'll see you later."

We went to a general practitioner, and the moment I undressed, I could see the shock in his eyes. He asked numerous questions. "You need to see a skin specialist; I'll book you into a hospital."

A week after, I was discharged and dragged myself to my niece's tenth birthday party wrapped in bandages. I had to wrap both my arms and legs in cling wrap and bandages for two weeks to heal faster.

"Dude! We bought you sweet chili Doritos, your fave," my sister said as if she had rehearsed that line the whole night.

"Sorry, dude, the doctor put me on an egg, meat, vegetable, water, and peanuts diet for five months! She says it's until the body gains enough fat for the skin to recover. Even the ointment she gave me smells like fat cakes. So, no Doritos, cool drink, cake, or scrumptious cookies today."

Having to arrive at a pool party looking like a mummy doesn't cut it. But you should have seen the glow on my niece's face at my arrival. I sure did make a hell of an entrance.

It was refreshing to see how nonjudgmental the little ones were. Everything seemed normal. The bandages "disappeared," and I felt normal around them. They are carefree souls. *We need more of those in this world, the world would be a better place, and people would have fewer suicidal thoughts and get through life much better without the criticism and stigma. Emotions eradicate willpower, so it's wise to keep them in check.*

The week before I was admitted was stressful due to mid-year exams. All that stress created a flare-up in my life. I woke up with a heavy and aching body; I hid it from my family by wearing long-sleeved T-shirts and pants. Not even my twin sister, whom I share a room with, saw it. Day after day, my cheeks seemed bigger than they were the previous day. My eyes shrunk more and more, and so did my confidence. They were heavier and more afraid of the light.

"Wow, other kids are losing weight during exam time, and you're gaining. You must be stress-free!" said my late physics teacher as he saluted. In South Africa, we salute to show respect or to show that you're the man! He was simply saying I was the girl and had my stress levels in check. *Little did he know.*

Eczema almost landed my mother in jail for assault, and I don't blame her. We were shopping, and on that day, I decided to wear a short, white clubwear summer playsuit with a pair of gorgeous red heels; a group of friends walked past us and stopped to stare at my flared-up, red, and itchy skin. One of them wanted to take a picture, not of how beautifully I was dressed but of my "perfect" skin. My mother made intense eye contact and furrowed her brows towards the guy with the camera, but at the same time, her eyes welled up with tears. I could sense how helpless she felt—she felt as if she couldn't protect me from this cruel world.

"Leave them; it's fine. It's not worth it," I said as I stopped Mom from confronting them.

Having to deal with skin issues as a teenager is one thing, but having to tolerate weight fluctuations is another psychological factor on its own! I had a bit of a break in the tenth grade: I wore whatever I wanted to, I enjoyed the temperatures that all the seasons offered, I was off to a new school, and I even went to the extent of being the overall top achiever in that grade. Life was good for me until the workload and complexity of the work increased in the eleventh grade. Within a few months, I gained 25 pounds (ca. 11 kg). The skin stored extra fat to protect itself from thinning further, and I was covered with a thick layer of rough, crocodile-looking skin. I worried about how I looked due to the weight gain and about how I would get rid of a whole 25 freaking pounds! Mind you; sweating is bad for eczema. So, no exercise for me! I was stuck. Should I continue with my exams and move on to the next grade, or listen to my body and give up?

I feel we live in predisposing times, where others treat people having illnesses with a different notion, bringing them to low self-esteem and less, or no, self-love. It's something that would have occurred if I had let it happen.

There were times I felt like giving up on myself, and some when I was so happy, I forgot about my health issues: the eczema, heart condition, and kidney failure.

Just when I thought the worst was over, I found out I had kidney failure after I collapsed in front of my examination room. If I had known better, I would've noticed that the constant urination was a red flag. That only lasted for about a month or two, thank the Lord!

Here I am a few years later, and I've never been better. I still have eczema, but it doesn't bother me that much. I go out more, and I wear whatever I want. I eat anything I want; everything! The doctor said I recovered pretty well, so I was allowed to do a few exercises. I dropped 26 pounds (ca. 12 kg). I've managed to get rid of the voice that always pointed out how damaged my skin was instead of telling me how beautiful and unique I am.

"Wow, you look great, and your skin looks far better than I had anticipated; in fact, it looks great. You're looking so beautiful!" My doctor said as I walked in for my appointment. I was shocked, and she completely caught me off guard.

"Really, Doc?" I wore a smile on my face; I felt like I had done something right; for the first time, I was in check, confidence-wise.

"So tell me, what do you do? Coz I can clearly see you take good care of yourself."

I didn't see that one coming—trust me—I thought it was going to be one of those dull in and out appointments.

"Oh no, nothing much. I just stay away from the sun and bathe with lukewarm water. When I have flare-ups, I put damp cloths over my skin and moisturize after."

"Wow, you go, girl! That's great. I'm not against any of that."

Damn! I felt in charge. My doctor changed my life and perspective. She made me realize that eczema is not the end of the world by sharing some of her skin-related struggles, which stunned me since she has the most radiant skin. I went home that day and saw a different person in the mirror.

The self-condemnation veil was removed; it was a wake-up call. I started affirming myself every day: "You're beautiful. You are wonderfully and fearfully made, and there's nobody else who can replace your personality and aura, girl. You're freakin' awesome!" My appointments are a breath of fresh air, and I always have conversations to look forward to. I couldn't wait to tell my doc about how I managed to publish my first book, *The Fifth Door,* without having many anxiety attacks or flare-ups.

Yes, the eczema has left a few scars, both physical and psychological, more than the kidney failure and heart condition have caused, but they don't define me or control my future.

Anxiety and anger diverted me from taking my meds as prescribed, but the moment I realized that they're not the enemy, everything changed. I stopped labeling them as the enemy and made them my friends. Having mastered the triggers of my flare-ups, I tried to prevent them as much as I could. If I have to do stressful work or go through deadlines, I meditate in prayer, take a deep breath, and just take a moment to remind myself that it's not part of God's plan for me to suffer, and nothing defeats me, nothing!

If you cannot be happy within yourself first, the world and everyone in it will be your enemy. We don't all carry the same load. Some have financial challenges, others have family problems or identity confusion, and some have medical conditions. I realized if I didn't work on myself, I wouldn't grow spiritually or psychologically, and if that happened, the young women who looked to me as their role model would, in turn, let go of themselves. Luckily the love I have for myself, and God was my strength and guide to change how I saw myself.

THE PRACTICE

EXPERIMENTAL ACCEPTANCE

No matter how cliché it may sound, the first step to healing will always pass through the stage of acceptance. It will do you no good to deny that you're different from others. Truth be told, your illness makes you stand out. Whether it be as visible as eczema or non-visible:

- Acknowledge that you are sensitive.
- You have a mission, and a purpose through your illness/es, to help others as well.
- Affirm yourself every day. Look yourself in the mirror and tell yourself, you got this! You'll pass through it.
- Search for people or that specific person who has gone through the exact type of illness. Search for the ones who are in the same age range as yourself. This can be from any source, and it can be from the Bible, a local newspaper, medical or health-related articles, or even better, someone you know of. Let's take a 19-year-old lady suffering from breast cancer as an example. What happened when she found out she had breast cancer? How did she bring herself to be emotional, physical, psychological, and spiritual acceptance? What went through her mind the first time she found out, and how did she feel about people's opinions?

FOCUS ON YOURSELF

"Ewwww, is that real?" People always have a mouthful to say, but it shouldn't bother you. They will have the nastiest looks to give, go to their homes, tell their families about you, and have a laugh or two, but after a day, you will be old news. What's left for you to do is:

- Let go of the words they have spoken, the nasty looks, the posted pictures, and indirects.
- Ignore them, or else you will go crazy!
- Prioritize your health over being a social feed.
- Be happy, regardless.

- Never be ignorant of taking medication; it's only until you are well.

- Stick to the doctor's instructions, and do everything by the book.

- Know the difference between faith for healing and ignorance.

Some illnesses disrupt emotions; they cause stress and anxiety. More especially if you know you have to do the same thing every day, it can be taking medication or following a strict diet.

"Unfortunately, I think depression and anxiety are really hard to live with. And what people don't need is to feel bad about themselves because they decide to go on medication." - Rene Russo

Refer to :
https://www.amazon.com/Complete-Guide-Psychological-Spiritual-Growth-ebook/dp/B0B6JS1FBM/ref=mp_s_a_1_1?

No matter how much you may struggle with your health, always focus on the bright side of things. It's not easy, but doable. Never wish you were somebody else. Someone out there also wishes they were you!

Nolwazi Charmaine Nkosi is a young lady from South Africa. She is an author of *The Fifth Door,* and a content writer at Monomousumi services; she has won several awards with them: two outstanding essay awards and an editor's choice award. She was published in the weaver magazine, volume 15 issue with the article: "Cooking versus baking." Furthermore, she has been openly writing since the age of 18. She started off with writing competitions like Short-Story.Me, and fortunately got published with them—that's where her writing career shot for the stars.

She started receiving recognition from many publishers who had impressive criticism for the quality of her writing, one of which is FunDza publishers in South Africa: "As a writer who is fairly acquainted with the works of people like Shakespeare and other such writers, it was refreshing to read a story with a similar motif as theirs but from a different perspective. It is not every day that one comes across a story about Western-style royalty, written from an outside perspective, and it was truly refreshing to read a story that makes it sound so fairly new. From the first line of your story, it was easy to tell that you have a great command of the written language, and your creative abilities shined through all the way to the last sentence. You are, without doubt, a brilliant writer, one whose talent is bound to grow from here on, and we are looking forward to reading more stories from you in the future."

In her spare time, she enjoys spending quality time with her family, cooking, and baking for them. She adores reading mystery novels, one of which is *The Adventures of Sherlock Holmes* by Arthur Conan Doyle.

Connect with Nolwazi:

LinkedIn: https://www.linkedin.com/in/nolwazi-nkosi-644b37221

Facebook: https://www.facebook.com/profile.php?id=100081889187683

Instagram: https://www.instagram.com/nolwazi_ nkosi

CHAPTER 15

INTO THE ABYSS

FINDING LIGHT IN THE DARKNESS

Billie Rinehart

MY STORY

Into the Abyss. . .I Go Again!

"Sometimes the bad things that happen in our lives put us directly on the path to the best things that will ever happen to us."

~ Nicole Reed

Abyss: a deep, immeasurable space, gulf, or cavity; vast chasm. Anything profound, unfathomable, or infinite: the abyss of time.

From a very early age, as far as I can remember, I was in situations completely unknown and uncomfortable to me. I call these times going into the abyss because, as a young girl, it felt like I was swung into a bottomless dark place where I had no idea how to land or what to grab on to. Being extracted from the nucleus of my family and everything familiar to me was like pulling the rug out from under my feet.

Learning to trust my caretakers and let go of my attachments (home and family), as well as learning to trust the people who created my safe environment, was imperative for my survival.

MY FIRST ABYSS

I'm seven years old. This house is dark and humid and smells old, like wood from a hundred years ago that has absorbed the thick humidity so characteristic of this tropical, wet country. I can hear my grandma out in the backyard yelling at the dog. I know I'm safe because Mama Bella, as I used to call her, was in charge of me now. Still, I feared the days ahead. *How did I get here? Why am I here? All I know is I want my mommy.* All of this just kept circling in my head.

"You will be going to a much better school now," my daddy explained while I looked up to him with eyes engulfed in tears and a big rock stuck in my throat that wouldn't go away.

I know my parents had the best intentions. I know it broke their heart not to have me at home with them. I didn't see it then, but I sure see it now. They trusted me. They saw my strength when I didn't. They saw a bright future ahead of me. They had the vision to plan and sculpt my life carefully. And for that, I'm eternally grateful.

My parents sent me to live with my maternal grandmother. Back then, we lived in my dad's hometown, which was so small, that it only had one public school. I'm the oldest of five children and the first one sent off to a better school in the city, which was just a bigger town with private schools.

My parents were always big believers in giving their children the best education money could buy. At the time, my grandmother, the most beautiful soul I've ever known, was like a mother to me. She showed me how to be loved. She taught me to be strong and independent and gave me the tools I needed to succeed. To this day, her advice rings as accurate as it did then, if not more. "You are the treasure. It is up to you, and only you, who gets to share it. Protect it with all your might" was my favorite advice and became my mantra throughout life.

I remember a lot of sad days during those years. When my dad visited, he sometimes left a shirt, pants, or a handkerchief behind. Latino men are notorious for wearing lots of cologne, and my dad always smelled so good!

I would hold that piece of clothing tight to my face breathing in his scent. His clothes smelled like love because when he hugged me goodbye, I could smell his clothes soaked in the familiar blend of spice, floral, and a hint of citrus. It felt like he was next to me as I sat holding his clothes to my face and crying myself to sleep.

Here I was, a scared seven-year-old, freshly yanked out of my comfort zone, away from my younger siblings and the simple sweet life of a small town where I freely went puddle jumping after a hard rain or ran free in the park in front of our house.

My parents explained that this arrangement was for my good, and one day I would understand the sacrifice they made by taking me away from my little brothers and sisters.

I attended a Catholic school in that town for the next six years. My grandmother was a retired teacher, so I was in great hands. She ensured I was well-fed, did well in school, and felt immensely loved. You know the saying, "I want to be just like you when I grow up?" Well, my grandmother made me feel precisely like that all my life. I have wanted to play that role more than anyone else—unconditional love at its finest.

Nonetheless, there was a massive hole in my heart I could not fill. The fear of not knowing if I'd ever see my family again took hold of every cell in my body. At seven years old, it's easy to imagine the worst. I did see them again, of course.

At some point during those years, the whole family moved to the town where I lived with my grandmother. My dad built a beautiful home for our family, where I lived happily for the next three years.

MY SECOND ABYSS

Rattled at 13, they sent me away, yet again, to a bigger city to attend one of the most prestigious Catholic schools in Panama.

This time, however, I was further away from my parents and siblings and living with my aunt and cousin in Panama City, Panama. The rug had been pulled from underneath my feet, again! My life felt like a big roller coaster with immense highs and big lows. There was so much to discover about who I was and how I was supposed to act. I was in survival mode, again.

Age 13 was a pivotal time in my life. I started to like a boy my dad disapproved of, so he handled it by separating us. Tears flowed down my face for days after losing my first puppy love. I was once again dealing with the separation from my parents, siblings, and my friends. I was the new kid in a new school, an all-girl private school where most girls had known each other since kindergarten. *Would they like me? Can I make some new friends? Am I smart enough? Pretty enough? Fun enough? Do I fit in?* I felt so lost and overwhelmed by it all. But it was, and still is, the best school in Panama. Remember: the best education money can buy!

Still, I wondered, *why can't I be home with my family? Why is my education so important?* My Abyss kept getting bigger. My fears also got bigger because my parents had to travel further to see me, so I would worry about them traveling safely.

Nonetheless, the days turned into months, and the months turned into years, and little by little, everything changed. I was a small-town girl living the big city life. Adapting to this new life propelled me into developing some severe resilience muscles and strong emotional maturity.

Four long years passed, and eventually, the city grew on me. So much so that I didn't feel like I belonged back in the small town I grew up in. The bond I developed with the girls I attended school with was so strong that some of us are close friends to this day. We couldn't help but establish close and lasting relationships since we went through our entire high school years with the same group of 50.

The small-town girl inside me started to disappear. The abyss took hold of her. My wings began to grow, and I believed I could fly.

My father thought so too. So, after graduating from high school and having a short visit at home, they shipped me off again. This time, to another country. The great USA!

MY THIRD ABYSS

At 19, freshly out of high school, I remember my dad standing in the doorway with a somber look on his face and saying, "I think you should go to the US and learn English because these days, everybody should be bilingual." My heart sank!

They picked LSU's program for its reputation for having one of the best English as a second language curriculums in the country.

Non-stop three and an a-half-hours flight from Panama to New Orleans. It sounded perfect. But here I was again, thrown into the abyss where I didn't speak the language and had no clue how to navigate through campus life or balance a checkbook. I was cold, nervous, and scared.

It was January, right smack in the middle of winter. I never owned a coat in my beautiful tropical country. I never experienced walking in the freezing rain to get to class or the cafeteria, where no one understood what I wanted to eat. I cried every single night. I begged to return home. My parents reassured me by saying, *"Nada es para Siempre, todo pasa y Tu Vida sera mucho mejor al final"* (This too will pass, and you will be all the better for it).

I remember looking out the window in my dorm room nine stories up and watching the rain hit the glass. I felt like a bird in a cage, longing to escape and fly back to a nest so far away. These were some of the loneliest times of my life—no one to talk to, nowhere to run. At this point, I spent more time away from my family than anyone I knew.

After my first semester, I passed the TOEFL (Test of English as a Foreign Language), a standardized test to measure the English language ability of non-native speakers wishing to enroll in English-speaking universities. I could read, understand, write, and even pass the test, but unfortunately, I could not speak a word. I was terrified to sound like a fool. Wouldn't anyone?

So, of course, my parents thought it would be best if I stayed for another semester and conquered spoken English. Eight months after my arrival in Baton Rouge, I dominated the language enough to attend college, which started a few weeks after finishing the English program.

By this time, my wings were fully developed and filled with beautiful colors. My college years were fun. So much so that I was saying "I do" at the altar instead of attending my graduation from college.

A year before graduation, I met a tall, dark, and handsome half French, half American green-eyed beautiful man who became the father of my two children.

Twenty years of marriage is nothing to sneeze at. We brought two beautiful children into this world; they are my pride and joy. But as life would have it, another abyss was in the cards for me—divorce.

MY FOURTH ABYSS

What now?! I was in my early forties and a stay-at-home mom with a 12-year hiatus on my resume. My mental to-do list looked something like this:

Must find a job.

Protect my two pre-teens (from the trauma of divorce).

Find myself.

Learn to balance a checkbook.

Kick fibromyalgia to the curb (No time for being tired and in pain all the time).

Find new friends (Sometimes, divorce can make friends disappear).

I cried every day for two years straight. I thought I'd never stop. *Where is my daddy? I wish he would tell me what to do. I'm in my forties. I'm not supposed to lose everything I worked so hard for. Wait! Maybe It was a bad idea to abandon the career my dad paid so dearly for.*

But the kids were my priority. *I did the right thing; I know I did. I need to figure out who I am now. Also, where will I find the strength to pick up the pieces and put myself together again?*

Sinking into the abyss again—this place looks familiar but unknown. It's a dark hole where nothing makes sense, and I didn't know which way was up. I looked for a glimmer of light coming from any direction. *Please, God help me!*

And then, the friends I least expected showed up as my light. They filled my heart with joy and sang the song of hope to me because I had forgotten the words. They shined their light on me, and I realized the wings were still there—a little bent but still functional.

I allowed my friends to become the wind beneath my wings. They supported me by believing in me and fueling my desire to succeed one way or another. It made sense to me at the time to follow my passion. So, that's what I did.

One of my close friends was an artist and offered me a job working at his art gallery in the French Quarter in New Orleans. How cool is that? Later, my stronger wings led me to accept a job as an interior designer for a boutique furniture store that also involved sales. Being scared paralyzed me and clouded my mind with doubt. I had to reinvent myself by stepping out of my comfort zone and visualizing myself as a warrior capable of conquering whatever challenges lay ahead—a strong version of me, just like that seven-year-old little girl who belonged to a family of seven but was always alone.

I then realized what my parents gifted me (besides the costly education). Every abyss in my path led me to this very moment. Every one of those experiences illustrated what courage felt like. Determination brought me to where I was at that moment. No, my story is not about abuse, neglect, or irreparable trauma. Mine is just a story about choices. The choices my parents made about my life, as well as the choices I made while navigating the unfamiliar and challenging times in my life. We all have options. Always. I chose to rise. I decided to conquer. I chose to grow. I chose love instead of fear. I chose calm instead of anguish. I trusted myself. I believed I could, so I did.

I have had an amazing, perfectly imperfect life; no regrets here. I'm eternally grateful for the vision my parents had for my life. The sacrifice they made to relinquish me to the world at such an early age. The dream my parents had for me turned out to be the dream life I always wanted.

Because of every change and challenge that came my way, I decided home is wherever I stand. My body is my temple. I am the universe experiencing itself. I am light. I am strength. I am love.

The trajectory of my life could have sent me on a tailspin, losing control and vision. The one thing I learned from all the uncomfortable situations I found myself in along my journey is that I was put on this Earth not just to survive but to thrive.

The abyss is nothing more than a place where opportunities for growth and change abound. They serve as a reminder to be fully present in order to find the force that resides within, so our gifts can be fully unlocked. Outside our comfort zone is where we find who we truly are. It's the place where we discover that fear is only holding us back from all that is possible. My life has been a long chain of leaps of faith. With every leap, I found a better version of myself I didn't know existed—every single time.

THE PRACTICE

GODDESS GATHERINGS
Using the Power of Women's Circles to Find Light in the Darkness

The comfort and happiness that genuine connection brings to your life is proof that in life, we're better together. We are here to help, support, and interact with one another.

The "Goddess Gatherings" I became a part of some years back have been a fountain of unconditional love, self-expression, and heartfelt support.

A gathering is a group of two or more. You pick the goddesses you want or need around you. Surround yourself with people who lift you and break down your walls or inhibitions. Goddess Gatherings are to bring women together in an intimate and loving sisterhood where everyone can feel free to share what lights them up.

It's time for a girl's night in! You might decide to:

Create a theme.

Cook together.

Dance.

Fill a bowl with topics to talk about.

Take pictures.

Do yoga.

Meditate together.

Catch a sunset together.

Go to a drum circle.

Hire an energy healer, make-up artist, etc., as a special guest.

The idea is to spark joy, raise your vibration, set yourself free, explore, be in the moment, share your light with others, and create a community of like-minded women who will elevate you and inspire you to embrace who you are and where you are in your life.

If you're not inclined to hang out with a group, or just moved and don't know anyone, or like me, lost friends after the divorce, you can try something new like yoga, a cooking or flower arrangement class, or even painting. Volunteering at a women's shelter is a great way to find connections and put yourself in a position to give.

"I have the power to create an explosion of magic in my life because I'm the keeper of my own gate, and I'm aligned with the life I want to experience."

~ Billie Rinehart

Billie was born in Panama, Central America, and is the oldest of five children. She arrived in the USA after graduating from high school and attended LSU to learn English as a second language.

After graduating from college, for the subsequent ten years, she practiced her degree in nutrition but found herself inclined to stay home and raise her two small children, a difficult decision that paid off tenfold because, thanks to her relentless dedication, her two children are now very successful thriving adults.

A stay-at-home mom for 12 years made Billie a perennial student and an avid reader, which helped her discover her passion for psychology, as well as cooking, gardening, and entertaining.

Billie has decided that the enormous wisdom and knowledge gained throughout her life would be best utilized by offering her services as a life coach, which she sees as an opportunity to help as many women as possible ignite the fire within and "Fill the pages in their stories with newfound purpose, courage, and excitement," she admits proudly. During her Goddess Gatherings, she has witnessed how easily and naturally women stepped into their greatness by simply checking their apprehensions and insecurities at the door, hence allowing their light to shine at its brightest and their spirit to flow in the beautiful space that is the now.

Her husband Todd is her best friend, boat captain, and partner in life who will go to the end of the universe to be by her side. Their current paradise is in beautiful sunny Florida.

"Today's mighty oak is yesterday's nut that held its ground."

~ Rosa Parks

Connect with Billie:

Email: billiestouch@yahoo.com

Instagram: @silvercrownmamacita

CHAPTER 16

RIP THAT BANDAGE OFF

HOW TO FACE YOUR PRESENT BY HEALING YOUR PAST

Lolita Guarin, Stress Management Expert

MY STORY

"I'm going to take a bike ride," my husband said confidently while putting his black sweatpants in his closet.

"Okay, and I'm going to the emergency room," I responded as I brushed my hair, stared at the mirror, and felt weak in my knees.

He stopped with one leg inside the sweatpants, looked at me, and reacted with a heightened tone of voice: "What kind of a controlling bitch you are that I cannot even take a bike ride by myself!"

"I am not telling you that you need to take me with you. I can go by myself. I'm just telling you where I'm going."

He finished putting his sweatpants on and tied his shoelaces in silence without even looking at me, rushing.

"I passed out on the kitchen floor last night because I'm bleeding so much. Since it's Sunday, I'm going to the emergency room by H-E-B." I reached for my mascara and continued with my eyelashes.

He didn't say anything after that. I felt a gust of air as he passed behind me and slammed the bathroom door as he left.

I collapsed on the kitchen floor the night before with a glass full of water in my hand. I remember falling down and my head bouncing off the cold tile as I met the floor. I cut my elbow on the glass as I fell. I don't remember how long I was unconscious, but it scared me enough to decide to check myself into the emergency room.

"I think you came right in time. If you waited till tomorrow, I think we would have needed to put you in the hospital," the doctor said to me. "How long has this been going on?" he asked me as he typed on the computer.

"This time, it's lasted for about three weeks, I think," I answered, staring at my phone, hoping to see a message or call from my husband.

"You need to see a specialist and take care of that." The doctor sighed and continued typing.

I remember my mother telling me as a teenager: "Be very careful while you're on your period. If you catch a cold, you can bleed to death, as I almost did in my thirties. Thank God your dad noticed something was wrong with me in the middle of the night and called the ambulance, or you would not have a mother right now." Well, I had a husband, but he could care less if I was dead or alive.

"How are you handling stress these days?" the doctor asked me.

"Uhm, well, like everybody else, I guess. Everybody is stressed out these days." I answered, smiling awkwardly.

"So, where is your stress coming from? Do you have work or family problems?"

I sat in silence, looking down at my red-painted toes. *Well, yes, I do, but who doesn't?* I thought.

For two years, I bled heavily during my periods, and they would last around three weeks. Somehow, I thought things would get better, and it would stop at some point on its own, like any other problem in my life. Well, it didn't, it just got worse, and my health deteriorated. I learned that stress has so much to do with our bodies, especially hormones, that it can be deadly for us women.

It took me another five years to realize I'd been living with a monster. No, not one who beat me or hurt me physically. He hurt me emotionally and mentally. What kind of husband does not take his wife to the emergency room? I think even a stranger would help another stranger in distress. But taking a bike ride was more important to him than taking care of his wife. I told my friends what happened to me, and I could see from their faces that whatever I was saying made them mad, no matter how much I tried justifying my husband's behavior.

I felt guilty for interrupting his day! My needs were not important. I was scared that he'd be angry and leave me. And what would I do if he did? Probably die! There were times during my marriage that I was miserable, but for the sake of looking good in front of others, "Until death do us part," and the fear of looking like a total failure in front of my parents, I continued to play my part.

Looking back, I can't believe how much I could endure and still think that life was not so bad. After all, other women were being beaten by their husbands every day. Emotional abuse leaves deep scars that take forever to heal, just like physical wounds. The emotional wounds are hidden under a fake smile. We're afraid to look at it, address it, and ask for help. It seems like everyone around us is doing so well, and we feel all alone with our problems—misunderstood.

I faced many issues in my marriage until, one day, I read a book about managing a business. The author shared her personal story of how she struggled with abandonment, fear, guilt, and low self-esteem due to being an adult child of an alcoholic. The concept was new to me, and I immediately picked up a book on that topic that she recommended and finished it within days. I couldn't believe what I was reading about! I recognized my struggle, insecurities, and fears.

Suddenly I understood that there was nothing wrong with me! My people-pleasing, abandonment issues, low self-esteem, fear, and anxiety were very common among adult children of alcoholics. It explained why I was still living with an abusive narcissistic husband!

I experienced childhood trauma, which still influenced my understanding of the world and how I relate and behave with others, especially in intimate relationships. However, what happened to me that day was not a once-in-a-blue-moon kind of experience with my ex-husband. No, that's how I was treated the whole 13 years of marriage: abandoned, laughed at, undermined, stonewalled, and gaslit, among other tools narcissists usually use.

Just like my needs were not significant when I was growing up, I allowed my needs not to be met in my marriage—simple needs of being protected, loved, honored, cherished, appreciated, and seen. I tried everything to be a perfect child or wife, but nothing worked! My friends asked why I still lived with him if he was treating me that badly. From my point of view, he wasn't treating me poorly. He was treating me normal. It was my normal not to be loved, appreciated, seen, or supported. Being hurt equaled being loved. The pain was equal to love. Because any interaction, any attention, even hurt, I took to heart.

Adult children of alcoholics are incredibly loyal, no matter how badly they're treated. They have a huge fear of abandonment and will please others just to be safe. They abandon their own needs to meet others' no matter the price they must pay and sacrifice themselves. That's what I did in my marriage. I married the same type of abusive man I grew up with. The saying that daughters marry the type of their fathers is true. I didn't believe that because my husband wasn't an alcoholic. But the abuse was the same.

I started a healing journey first by identifying what was happening to me and then acknowledging how it hurt me. I underwent surgery that took out a fibroid the size of a grapefruit, and my body felt much better. Then little by little, I was not scared to look at my needs and give myself support, compassion, care, and love. I learned how to care for myself, meet my needs, stand by my own side, and honor myself. I got out of marriage painfully, just like ripping off a bandage, but I did it. When I made up my mind, I just ripped it off. Do you have bandages to rip off?

You might also be suffering from childhood trauma and don't know it, especially if your caregivers forbid you to tell the truth. Maybe you were told that nothing leaves the family, and you should act like nothing is wrong. You might also want to please someone, so you stay abused in order "not to rock the boat." You might even have children and think you don't want them to grow up without a father or mother. You might have another relationship or a job you're staying in because you're afraid to move. It looks terrifying and unsafe. You might be thinking you'll die if you leave. But trust me, you can.

I want to share a process that is still helping me identify my childhood trauma so I can heal when it triggers me. And like any other process, it has the most impact on your life when used regularly. So don't postpone this. Instead, take time for yourself and your healing.

THE PRACTICE

Divide a piece of paper into two columns. On the left, list a problem or issue that you're facing. Or even any situation that doesn't make you feel good. You're looking for the feeling that something is wrong that makes you feel bad or negative. You might not even know what's wrong, especially if you're used to abuse.

If you can't pinpoint right away what's triggering you in your current relationships, then just start listing the most important people in your life or others with whom you spend a lot of time. Then go one by one on the list and ask yourself what issues you usually encounter with them and how that makes you feel. I also recommend observing yourself next time you are around them. How do you feel? How do you talk? Do they invoke some specific sensations in your body? What about your tone of voice? Do you feel happy or sad around them? Maybe scared? If you grew up in an abusive environment, you might believe that whatever you're experiencing is normal and that you shouldn't complain about it. More than that, you might be feeling guilty about doing this exercise in the first place. Overcome the guilt and procrastination. Just observe yourself and record the situation in detail with neutral emotion. Pay attention to what your gut feeling is telling you.

Then on the right side of the paper, write down an event, situation, or feeling associated with what you experienced in the past. List as many memories as you can from your childhood.

After you're done, look at what you wrote in the two columns. Do you see the pattern between your past and present? Do you see that is why you behave the way you behave? It could feel customary to you, and any abuse might feel even deserved, especially if you grew up with an addict in your environment and your feelings were constantly ignored, undermined, and invalidated. So, if you get frustrated when your husband doesn't call you to tell you that he will be late for dinner, you get angry at him when he returns. But that is just fear of abandonment. That fear reminds you of your childhood, and you're projecting this experience to explain and make sense of things from the survival point of view.

When you identify your triggers, there are two ways to move past them. If you realize that you're experiencing mental or physical abuse, it's time to talk to a specialist about it, ask for help, or just leave the situation. If you realize many fears are coming from your childhood trauma, ask your family members, friends, and those you love to help you overcome them with patience and care. Come up with a plan for how you can soothe yourself. If you need help with that, please book a call by going to register at www.BeAmazingYou.com

Lolita Guarin is a passionate author, empowering speaker, and trustworthy coach for busy professionals and adult children of addicts. She is a licensed and certified stress management and life coach and author of the book *Crush Stress While You Work* and *Stress Management for Adult Children of Alcoholics.* She is also Reiki Master and certified lightworker. Lolita has been featured as a guest on the *Ask Dr. Nandi Show,* magazines, and many podcasts.

She is a founder of Be Amazing You, which provides coaching and online courses to lower burnout and increase energy and well-being. To teach stress management, Lolita has organized and facilitated online and in-person workshops for groups and individuals. In addition, she founded a membership that continues support to those who have suffered childhood trauma due to an addicted parent and others who suffer from burnout, low energy, and stress.

Lolita has dealt with stress and tried many stress-release techniques over the years as a busy professional and childhood trauma survivor. After her health deteriorated due to stress, she went on a quest to find a solution that consisted of natural remedies and practices. Managing stress without medication became her priority, and teaching that to others became her passion.

After years of researching stress relief techniques, attending workshops, coaching, and practicing on her own, she found a better and more natural way to battle stress than going on chronically depleted. And it starts with recognizing and healing childhood trauma as a precursor to how we deal with stress in general, which became one of the teaching pillars for managing stress.

Connect with Lolita:
Website: www.BeAmazingYou.com
Facebook: Follow Lolita on www.facebook.com/LolitaGuarin
Join private Lolita's Facebook group, just search for Stress Management for Adult Children of Addicts.

CHAPTER 17

BEING PRESENT IN THE MESS

A POWERFUL PRACTICE FOR THRIVING

Delores Tronco

MY STORY

My sharpest memory of that time is the feel of cold linoleum under my feet and the buzz of florescent lights shining from above. I follow the nurse down the corridor to the operating room and through the door. Inside, the fluorescent lights intensify, and the temperature is 20 degrees colder. I feel tiny and helpless, like an ant sizzling under a magnifying glass in the hands of some careless, sociopathic eight-year-old.

"If you'll just climb up on the operating table," she says. The stainless steel of the table is icy, and my hospital gown twists uncomfortably beneath me as I lie down. I wonder briefly why a hospital would require a patient to walk into surgery. I internally picture an inmate walking to execution, one dreaded footstep in front of the other, and wonder briefly if being forced to walk is some fresh new hell I'd entered.

For a fleeting moment, I think, *the restaurant opens the day after tomorrow, and absolutely everything is on the line,* and then the anesthesiologist leans over my face and says a bit too cheerfully, "Now, just begin to count down from ten, and we'll see you on the other side." I get to six, and the room grows dim, sweet oblivion enveloping me in darkness.

Several hours later, I awaken to a male nurse checking for bleeding between my legs. I'm hazy enough from the drugs to feel only mild revulsion and self-consciousness when my situation registers. "I want to sleep," I say and turn my head away, trying to forget that it's losing a baby that brought me to this hospital too soon, long before the joyful delivery I'd imagined.

The pregnancy had come as a surprise nine weeks earlier. My husband and I stared at the pregnancy test in astonishment. We hadn't been trying, and a period of disordered eating and excessive exercise in my twenties left me concerned that it would be difficult to conceive later in life.

The fact that we were about to open a restaurant in Manhattan's famed West Village just nine weeks later only added to our shock and apprehension about the pregnancy. Three years prior, I sold my first restaurant, Work & Class, in Denver, hell-bent on making it in New York. I wanted to take a step back from ownership to become a student of hospitality in the greatest city in the world; then, when it was time, to open a restaurant and prove that I could succeed in what is arguably the most difficult market in the country.

And I loved New York—loved it like a hopelessly romantic teenage girl with a fervent high school crush. Despite its flaws, inconveniences, and propensity to foster a Stockholm-Esque syndrome in its inhabitants, I could see only its beauty, energy, and soul. As a teenager who never quite fit into the cliques of my small-town high school, New York City was a revelation. My intensity and predilection for speaking my mind, the speed I naturally walked with, and the banter that rolled so naturally off my tongue (kibitzing, my father called it) all made me a natural fit in the city. For the first time, I felt seen, accepted, and loved as though I'd found the long-lost soulmate I'd been searching for my whole life.

And yes, as anyone will tell you, having a baby in New York City is no piece of cake. If you've ever seen an exhausted mother struggling to lug a stroller, child, and baby bag up and down the subway stairs, you know precisely what I'm talking about. Everything also costs more in New York, and space comes at a premium. Nursery, what nursery? Do you mean our walk-in closet?

Adding to the list of potential challenges was that in just a few short weeks, everything I dreamed of professionally was on the verge of coming to fruition. As any restaurateur worth their salt will tell you, you get one chance to open. Blow it, and you've blown your shot at success and recognition, and I wanted both.

For the last three years, I'd taken a sizable demotion from my previous owner status. I waited tables in the East Village, trying to creatively convey the merits of New-Hungarian-American food to our guests. I schlepped from Brooklyn to midtown for classes at the International Wine Center. I worked as an assistant to one of the owners of New York's famed Blue Hill and Blue Hill at Stone Barns, a mercurial man who swung from telling me I would become the female Danny Meyer to asking loudly enough for my office mates to hear, "How stupid can you possibly be?"

I endured it all, and amid all of that, I convinced a West Village landlord to take a chance on a girl from Colorado, raised $1.6 million in investment, and conceptualized, designed, and built a restaurant. Now here I was, newly pregnant and mere weeks from opening. The restaurant would be called The Banty Rooster; in honor of the nickname my Nebraskan turned Coloradan mom gave me as a kid. Bantam roosters are the smallest in the farmyard, yet through a combination of determination and sharp elbows, they often rule the roost. Just like a bantam, I'm small in stature but full of heart, big ideas, and an underdog's determination to make it against all odds.

So just like many women throughout history who have done what had to be done, I went into planning mode. When the baby was born, I would wear her in a carrier on my chest, I reasoned, and pump in the office before dinner service. We'd figure out part-time childcare since that was all we could afford, maybe even find another couple in our enormous apartment building for a nanny-share. It would be worth it because we'd be joyfully welcoming a new life into the world.

Most mornings during that time, I jog along the waterfront in Brooklyn, talking to the baby along the way. I resolutely eliminate coffee and alcohol from my diet. In my mind, the baby is a girl whom we will name Eva Noel. I tell her about all the adventures she'll have as a kid in New York City. I dream of taking her to Broadway shows, MOMA, Yankees games, and the city's greatest restaurants, exposing her to all the art and culture I didn't have access to in my childhood. I begin to love her with a fierceness I can't fully describe—a protectiveness and selflessness I've never experienced before.

Six weeks after the fateful pregnancy test, my husband and I leave the restaurant for our first ultrasound appointment on the Upper West Side. I dress up a little—maybe I want the doctor to think well of me, or perhaps it feels like a special occasion. On the train ride uptown, I picture leaving the office with a strip of those black and white in-utero photos and plan to hang one on our refrigerator.

In the nurses' station, they take my blood pressure and weight. I'm up three pounds, which makes me proud instead of panicky for the first time in my life. Afterward, the nurse takes us to an exam room and asks me to remove everything below the waist and cover myself with a paper blanket.

A few minutes later, the doctor enters the room. Chit chat follows. And then, the moment I'd been waiting for comes—the ultrasound. Out comes the wand, and inside me it goes, uncomfortable, cold, and sticky. On the screen, my insides are projected in black and white, staticky like an old television tuned to a channel you don't pay for. I gaze at the screen and hold my breath.

"Hold on a second," the doctor says. "Just looking around, and. . ." she trails off and sighs. "I'm so sorry, but there isn't a heartbeat."

I turn my head to look at my husband and feel my soul detach from my body, the depersonalization of dissociation taking over.

Suddenly, I'm floating above the exam table, watching a petite woman and her husband talk to the doctor below. The doctor explains that it's a silent miscarriage, which means that the fetus has stopped growing. Even though the woman did not bleed and was still experiencing all the symptoms of early pregnancy—morning sickness, fatigue, changing hormones—the pregnancy was over. There are three options. The woman can wait to see if the tissue and blood pass on their own, take a pill that will move things along but could land her in the emergency room if the bleeding and pain are too much, or have a surgery called a dilation and curettage to remove the uterine lining and tissue.

The next 24 hours are a blur. I schedule the surgery for December 9— the tiny break between friends and family services on December 5, 6, and 7 and the public opening on December 11. I return to the restaurant to gather a few belongings and burst into tears when my assistant manager asks about the appointment. My husband, grieving in his way, shuts down and says only that he thought I worked too hard, inferring that somehow, the opening of the restaurant or I had caused the miscarriage. In retrospect, I know it wasn't his intention to be cruel, but cruel it was, and deep it cut.

That night, I go home to our 800-square-foot apartment and come unglued. I weep ugly, guttural sobs—the kind that makes you gasp for air—the likes of which I hadn't experienced since my father's passing six and a half years prior. I sit on my living room couch clinging to my beloved dog Macy and tell myself that this is the last time I can lose it, that I must pack the sadness up and put it in a box on the shelf until the restaurant opening is over. Even in my immense grief, I feel I owe it to myself and my team to show up fully.

I'm thankful that I didn't know then what was coming. Ninety-six days after our opening on December 11, 2019, COVID-19 came roaring through New York City, more destructive than any hurricane or terrorist attack. Faced with a landlord who would not bend on our $23,000 per month rent, I fought tooth and nail to save my beloved Banty Rooster, but in the end, I lost the fight. Worse yet, I was saddled with a significant SBA loan from the restaurant's opening.

Later that year, my marriage crumbled under the weight of my husband's secrets. It was too broken to save, so I gathered my strength and left, heartbroken and discouraged, alone and afraid.

Seemingly surrounded on every side by challenges beyond my control, I took one painstaking step at a time. I cried until I couldn't cry anymore. I went to therapy. I filed for divorce. I began planning a new restaurant in Colorado. I recruited a chef from New York City and moved him across the country. It wasn't easy, but in just over a year from when The Banty Rooster closed, I successfully conceptualized, designed, and built a new restaurant. Named The Greenwich in honor of New York City's Greenwich Village, the restaurant opened on September 30, 2021.

For more than two years, I stood in the middle of the mess—the chaos that descended on my life regardless of whether I deserved it or not. A mess can be literal, physical chaos, like the aftermath of a natural disaster, or intangible, like the emotional chaos of grief, hurt, and unmet expectations. Mine was both. Sometimes you get yourself into the mess, and sometimes the mess shows up unannounced on your doorstep, stubbornly refusing to leave.

Surviving this period and rebuilding my life—something that required my best and highest functioning self—taught me some important lessons, the most vital of which I call "being present in the mess."

THE PRACTICE

The first step to being present in the mess is acknowledging that messes are inevitable. Life is complex, and so are human beings and relationships. Finding yourself in a mess does not necessarily reflect poor choices or failure on your part—sometimes, we get there as a result of other people's actions or forces beyond our control. People we love age and get sick, and sometimes they die. We and the people we love develop and battle addictions. We experience traumas that we carry with us for years to come. We get into car accidents, accept jobs that turn out to be nightmares, and sometimes unwittingly draw the short straw in the game of life.

Embrace that avoiding the mess altogether is impossible. Some people live their entire lives diligently, trying to avoid any discomfort. They try to control the uncontrollable, refusing to take risks. They wall off their emotions and bury their vulnerabilities six feet under, hoping they'll never find the light of day. God forbid someone says they are "too much" and things get messy—it's all about appearances. Here's the problem—appearances aren't real. Hiding a mess doesn't vanquish it. They are inevitable, as much a part of life as our successes and accomplishments.

The second step to staying present in the mess is grounding ourselves. To do this, I start by connecting with my five senses. *What can I see, feel, hear, taste, and smell right now?* I might notice the humming of a fan, birds chirping, or the buzz of conversation. Maybe I see the shape of the leaves on the tree outside my window or a piece of artwork I've never really studied. I might smell cookies baking or the freshly cut grass outside or feel my sweater's softness and the radiator's warmth next to my desk. All these ordinary things have an innate beauty and stand to ground us in the present.

The third step is prayer. Prayer is the acknowledgment that I cannot do it on my own. It is not weakness, nor is it talking to the molecules in the air. When I pray, I start with *Dear God, here I am again.* People claim that they can't believe in a God they can't see, to which I think, *Can you see or touch love?*

The point here is not the existence or nonexistence of God, but reliance on something greater than me. It's saying thank you, even in the mess. It's asking for strength when I can't stand on my own. It's stepping out in faith, taking tangible steps that say, *I don't know what I'm doing, so I surrender. Please guide my path and show me the truth.*

The fourth step is visualization. On the worst days, I picture myself lying on a beach as waves crash over me. Sometimes the waves lap at my feet, gently licking at my toes. Other times, they crash so hard and fast that I can barely breathe. The intensity can be physically uncomfortable, making me want to crawl out of my body and do something, anything, to numb the pain. In those moments, I remind myself that tides rise and fall, but eventually, the waves always recede. The same is true of emotions—even the rawest and most painful emotions cannot last forever. They pass, and when we allow ourselves to remain present for them, we learn that we're stronger and more resilient than we ever imagined. By remaining present for the full range of our emotions, we clear out space for new experiences, relationships, and growth.

The final step is sharing the mess with others. As humans, we're built for community. Being candid about our struggles and vulnerabilities takes them out of the dark and into the light, where they often seem less daunting. If we live our lives constantly afraid of being judged, we risk never connecting with others in a meaningful way. And who knows? Talking about your mess might comfort or encourage someone else to share their struggles or persevere in the face of difficulty. Show up. It may be uncomfortable, but so is keeping it pent up inside.

And that says it all. Showing up is another way of saying you're present in the mess. First for yourself, and then for others. It's a practice that has taken me through my darkest times, and I venture that it will take me through others. Breathe in, breathe out, and imagine the waves crashing. They'll always recede.

Delores Tronco is the CEO and founder of The Greenwich, a lively, ingredient-driven new American restaurant in Denver's RiNo neighborhood.

A natural entrepreneur, Delores' previous restaurant credits include the nationally acclaimed Work & Class, the short but sweet Banty Rooster, and Denver pop-up The Justice League of Street Food. She is also a WSET III sommelier and graduate of The International Wine Center in Manhattan.

Her daily mission is to create an inspiring and nurturing environment for her guests and staff by making food, wine, and hospitality accessible and fun for all. She is passionate about developing leadership skills in her team and hopes to leave the hospitality industry better than she found it. Delores also shares her expertise through her consulting practice on a variety of topics, including restaurant openings and operations, leadership development, bar and wine programs, and more.

Connect with Delores:

Website: https://www.delorestronco.com or www.thegreenwichdenver.com

Linked In: https://www.linkedin.com/in/delorestronco/

Instagram: https://www.instagram.com/delores.tronco/

Facebook: https://www.facebook.com/delores.tronco/

CHAPTER 18

PAIN IS YOUR POWER

BROKEN BUT FREE

Amber Jace

MY STORY

They both heard and felt my spine crunch. Their dad's knee is on my neck as I lie on my back on top of a footrest. The crunch has set off a wail of cries. Screaming, "No, stop!" Our fighting escalated when we moved to his hometown on his reservation. We were married for almost nine years. We're both Shoshone; he is also Bannock.

The reservation life is, as one may guess, a place where you don't have to travel too far to bump into a home with alcohol abuse. He and I had this in common, though his experience was on a much deeper scale than I imagined existed. Each generation on the reservation is dealing with this less and less; I can speak of this in regards to my own reservation. I know my parents dealt with drunk parents on a consistent basis. Whereas my generation, if you didn't have an alcoholic parent, then birthdays and holidays are where you would find the action. In my own experience, both my father and stepfather were addicted to the drink. They were two different drunks—opposites, really. My stepfather was a rage addict and would yell consistently. My father, on the other hand, was a happy drunk; he lived 15 minutes away but was only around to tell stories.

When I look back on my relationship with my ex-husband, listening and trusting intuition should've been easy. But in those life-changing moments, I had chosen not to be brave nor courageous. Not listening to that voice telling me to say something, to think twice. I know I had doubt; I can see it on my face in the pictures of our courthouse nuptials. I watched myself go through the steps. Building up our relationship in my head long before we ever got together. You could say I manifested this relationship, my version of the ideal.

We were very young when we met, only in the fifth grade. We were both on traveling basketball teams. On most reservations, basketball tournaments are a big event. Tribes travel to each other's reservations to play. Me being from Nevada, and him from Idaho. This is how we met, and from that moment on, I thought, wrote, and daydreamed about this individual. This went on for years, even after his phone was shut off from the many long-distance calls. I adored the idea of him; it was my happy place. My home life growing up was full of rage and yelling, traits I had to learn to release.

Eleven years later, at a basketball tournament, we met eyes and were inseparable, although the fairytale grew gray quite quickly. *Do you hear that?* There was that voice again, telling me he keeps doing those things that are literal red flags. He lied about everything, and it made no sense to me why. I always had an ability to detect lies within words spoken. I didn't keep in mind what he lied about, only a running tally of how often it's happening.

This relationship started when we were 21 and in a party phase. Countless bar fights and leaving me home while he sat in the drunk tank. But when I took the chance to go out with my friends, he immediately latched to any conclusion of deceit. I didn't cheat on him, though sometimes I wish I had. There were many arguments over this subject, year after year, month after month, day after day. The arguments weren't just yelling. He allowed himself to go to a place inside of him where it was okay to put his hands on me.

Pumping himself up to turn red, yelling, "You cheat on me?! Fuck around on me?!" Pinning me in a corner, he choked me, pushed me around, turned my legs black and blue, and laid on top of me, so I stayed put while he yelled in my face. At times when I defended myself and hurt him in the process, he would freak out and be livid with me for days on end. We have three children together, and each of them has a memory of abuse—a heart-wrenching fact we're currently healing through.

I've been a mom since 18 and started working right away. My oldest son is from a previous relationship, another that left me feeling unworthy. To be cheated on multiple times, including with friends. What a twisted rabbit hole of undesirable thoughts of self-worth. The irony after leaving my oldest son's dad was that my ex-husband happened to be faithful, but that wasn't enough.

When my ex started working for my stepdad, it turned into both of them drinking daily. It was my childhood all over again. I was in fear of the sound of truck tires pulling into the driveway. I couldn't sleep all night for fear. Did someone piss him off? Did he lose money? Repeated bad outcomes awaited me. I had to handle the drunk husband, whose anger could be lit like a lighter. If he was in a mood to argue, then it was on and could last days.

It was in a dark place where writing and poetry slowly brought me light. I didn't think of myself as a writer. I've always had a tendency to write in a dyslexic manner. Let's say many rough drafts there are. Life brings out our natural gifts in the most unexpected ways.

What I share now is not something I share with ease but a part of my story nonetheless. We decided to go out with friends one night. Not being out in a year, we were more than a little tipsy. At the end of the night, we got into a cab together to go home but argued. I got out of the cab and walked home, and he went back to the bar. On my way home, I stopped at a gas station to grab something to eat for the walk. A friend of a friend noticed me; he was standing with a woman, "Hey, need a ride home?" he said. "No, I am good," I replied.

I paid, walked outside, and there they were, begging to give me a ride. "Hey girl, I can't let you walk home. Just get in the car." They both exclaimed. I declined over and over but failed and got inside of the car. The woman was blabbing her mouth as she offered her drink to me repeatedly. Annoyed, I took a sip and pointed out my house.

As you might guess, this did not end well. The friend of a friend came back to my house with a male friend and raped me. I was not conscious and do not remember, but this is how the men bragged of it later. I was awoken by my ex-husband's hands gripped tightly around my neck, him yelling in my face while I gasped for breath. I was in a daze trying to recall the evening. *I didn't cheat; where are my clothes? I didn't cheat!*

I explained who had given me a ride home, but he didn't believe me. I walked into stores for months peaking behind my own back, wondering what I'd say if I ever saw this man or if I saw the other walking around. I didn't know what he looked like. I was sick to my stomach and cried myself to sleep every night. *Why hadn't I gone to the police?* I wished over and over that I wasn't so naïve. But more importantly, wished my husband would protect me instead of blaming me. This happened a year after I had my third son, and it sent me into a deep depression. I refused to speak.

My ex hid this from everyone and had to take on all my roles in the house. While I was not talking, I started writing—nothing poetic yet, nothing that made me light up. The opposite actually, I started writing all of the terrible thoughts swimming around inside my head. This notebook I hid from any peeking eye was beginning to fill up. *If anyone had the chance to read it, they might think me a monster.* But I was never a monster. I was broken, and healing, and broken, and healing. I can remember the day I threw out the notebook. I smiled a real smile and made the choice to start speaking again for my children. Yet I still had not chosen to leave their father. That choice was always on my mind, though I had no idea how to execute it.

In our relationship, I kicked him out of the house a few times and called the cops on him a few times. This left me with damaged family ties and a home full of holes in the walls. I was ashamed of my home and didn't want anyone to see what I let happen.

I then fell into a routine. I had a good job and could afford to give us the things we wanted, which wasn't much. We're accustomed to less. This was when I started to indulge in smoking weed. I'm an advocate for the benefits of cannabis, but weed was my addiction of choice. I smoked weed to numb those voices in my head that wanted so badly for me to get out of this relationship. I smoked to be numb, and I became addicted to being numb.

I would wake up every morning before the sun and be sure to look professional. My routine was my comfort zone. By this time, my ex-husband had quit drinking. One day he decided he wasn't going to do it anymore and didn't. He left behind drinking and picked up on the weed smoking. When he put down the drink, I thought that it meant less fighting. I was wrong. I was always wrong.

Waking to get ready in the morning was a buzz kill. I held a knot in my stomach for the fight I knew was coming. *If you tiptoe, you won't wake him.* A cheap mantra I rehearsed every morning.

"Who are you looking good for?" Like clockwork, he argued I was up to something. Timing me between locations and giving the silent treatment for time spent with family. Every argument built up like a volcano of bubbling fury. He had no reason to believe I was cheating, no proof. *Maybe if I go without a phone, he will see that I am trustworthy and honest.* For seven-plus years, I went with no phone, only in the beginning believing this would aid in his trust for me.

A delusional thought I convinced myself of. He simply turned that into an accusation that I was using my computer at work to cheat. If, for some reason, he showed up at my place of work. I was in immediate distress, on my toes, and prepared for the allegation. I always hoped and wished he would rub his eyes one day, and when he looked at me, he'd actually see me. That day has not come, and I no longer wait for it.

At the beginning of covid, I thought of a plan to get away. No one was going to like this plan. My acting skills would be tested. *If he catches on, he will surely make his own plan to kill me.*

The plan was to move. My ex-husband's family home in Idaho has acres of land that were once used for farming alfalfa. His grandfather lives there and could use our help. We were getting a good refund from my tax return, so I suggested we leave. He was hesitant at first as he didn't want to live in his family home again. So, I drew up plans, made a to-do list, and pushed him on the subject daily. Finally, he agreed, and we upped and moved within a week's time, without really telling anyone. My family was worried for me in our hometown; leaving made it worse. But no shaking heads could knock me off course. *Remain confident, Amber. This is the way out; you got this.*

When we arrived in Idaho, we started our work on the yard and land. My children loved having animals and were outside more than at our home in Nevada. When my ex started working, his child support kicked in. He immediately started to feel the burden, and we could feel it too.

His attitude changed now that we were in his hometown. Consistently worried about what everyone else was thinking, his delusional thoughts took over, and we started fighting again. Only it was worse here. He had no shame here. Living in a home far from any ears, he hit me harder and yelled louder. Eyes bulging from his skull were my clue to the physical violence. He went further into that place, not stopping at the sight of blood. This happened a few times before I picked a date to leave.

Like any other day, I woke up and went to let the chickens out and feed and water the pigs. I then woke the kids up and got them ready for school, making sure my ex was getting ready as well. First, dropping the kids off at school, and then I dropped him off at work. A normal day, except it wasn't. His grandfather was still sleeping as I pulled into the driveway. Scared and anxious, I quickly started packing all of our clothes and blankets into the truck. I then called the school to let them know I'd be there to pick up my sons. They were not surprised to see our stuff packed. There was no time for goodbyes, just tears for the long-distance drive.

I admit I've not been the best parent I could be. It breaks my heart. My bad parenting choices have been a harsh reality, choices made that are now theirs to bare. After much reflection, I've forgiven myself, allowing freed up space inside to teach myself parenting technics learned online or through friends. I only wish the best for myself and the children I've been blessed with.

It's been two and half years since I left my ex-husband. Now I am able to rub my own eyes and see my story in its entirety. I was turning a blind eye for far too long. All of us are born with intuition, but along the way, making choices not to see. It's our path—to each their own, in time. I realized my power before leaving my ex-husband but was afraid to share it with him. He did not like for me to shine. Not many I've come across have. I almost believed their silence.

We all get many chances to choose an easy path or a hard one. I almost always chose the hard, thinking it was easy. Coming out of this habit we form of not feeling like we deserve better is so painful but worth every tear-drenched step. To feel your pain is your power. To make it through your hardest times, being wholeheartedly honest with yourself, digging through the unfinished business that lives inside your mind is your power. Releasing these emotions can mean suffering. The suffering that is needed.

The below three stages were crucial for me. I hope my story can help you begin or push further into healing. We are all one, in different phases.

THE PRACTICE

ISOLATION

Time in isolation forces a change in perspective. Time alone is adjustable to your own schedule. Take the time to heal and feel your pain. Away from social media and being social in general is needed. It's not easy and does get lonely. You can distract yourself with isolated activities. Meditate, go for a walk or run, to the garden, or sit outdoors. This will require a commitment to yourself. Asking yourself question after question. What role do we all play in each other's scenarios? Understanding point of view. Not always agreeing but understanding.

FORGIVENESS OF SELF AND OTHERS

To forgive ourselves and others is to release a burden that is not yours to hold. Think of the grudges you hold against yourself, anyone, or anything. Each one pulls you further from self. It's hard to believe that such could affect you, but it does, in fact. Negativity shouldn't be held long in your mind—it's a sickness. What's done is done; look forward, not back.

When working on understanding, please do not ask yourself. *What would I do if I were them?* Rather put yourself in their shoes and gain their perspective on the choice and decision made. Journaling can help aid in seeing the entire picture. Release what you cannot control and be honest regarding self. Forgiveness, once learned, will set you free.

INTUITION

In each case decision, we have the first thought. Now that first thought is almost always not easy. This is why we tend to ignore it or second guess.

When we do that, we are not following intuition. We are making a simple choice for now. A choice, whether it be saying yes to a hidden consequence or choosing to be with someone you like rather than someone you love. Neither is bad. It's simply us refusing to learn the first time, which will come back to us.

What comes with trusting intuition is walking confidently in all situations because you've done the work and are able to better see the entire picture of your truth—knowing the power within.

No experience is bad, and none of us are either. I believe this world we live in is full of magic. Magic that is real if you believe it is. I had to get through these obstacles and many more, it was meant to be, and you were meant to read this—light and love to you and all.

Amber Jace has not always been a writer. Her first ever job as a young teen mother led her into the accounting field. She started work for Coach USA, peeling stickers from the buses. They eventually invited her into the finance department to learn what would be her career for the next six years—working for finance departments at Elko Band Council and for Braemar Construction.

Amber is a member of the Te-Moak tribe of Western Shoshone bands of Indians. The tribe is located in beautiful northeastern Nevada. Amber is a proud descendant of the Newe Sogobi (The People of the Land). The horrific treaty singing history of her people led her to write. She wept her feelings onto paper as she wrote a poem about the tragic incident. Performing this poem at Elko, Nevada, National Cowboy Poetry Gathering—open mic. One handshake after another. She could not deny that within there was a talent with words.

Amber is a kind, funny, lighthearted woman. She has a way of being a great listener. For her, this is a superpower. To hear someone out fully without any regard to self, she claims, aids an individual's soul. A love for knowledge and the great outdoors. She can be caught hiking, reading, playing, and sharing a laugh with her four children.

Amber is currently working on a novel. A fantasy/non-fiction novel. She gives some detail about the journey her main character has begun. A tale that is close to home and intertwined with the stories of her culture and neighboring tribes. A young woman is transported back into the time before settlers. A big hairy manlike figure they call the traveler picked her up and threw her. Waking up naked on the side of a familiar mountainside. She must find a path.

Connect with Amber Jace:

Gmail: ambjace@gmail.com

TikTok: @ambjace

CHAPTER 19

THE BATTLE OF MENTAL ILLNESS TAKING OVER YOUR CHILD

FINDING A GLIMPSE OF LIGHT IN PURE DARKNESS

Tanya Garner

MY STORY

I was on the front porch, finally feeling at peace in every area of my life, when all of a sudden the phone rang; little did I know the news on the other end would forever change my life! As my mom, through quick breaths, frantically tried to explain something over the phone that was happening to my son, I heard her say, "Something is truly wrong; I think he's on drugs! It has to be some type of hard drug. He has to be high. I need you to help figure out what he's on."

I had just made a fresh start in life. As I rolled over, eyes adjusting to the morning sun, heart pounding with excitement, I started getting ready for the long drive ahead, finally leaving Minnesota in the rearview mirror and heading back home to Denver, where I longed to be. I quickly got my things set up, putting my office together in my grandma's old sewing room, organizing my bedroom and the bedroom my kids would call their own. Then, feeling a happiness I hadn't felt in years, I nestled into bed and fell fast asleep.

Even though I moved back to Denver to help care for my grandma, diagnosed with uterine cancer, this move was so much more than that to me. It was a new beginning, a fresh start, as they say. It was an outlet to finally walk away from a marriage that held me back from truly living my life. I put all my focus into raising my three kids. My kids were grown and graduated and finding their way, and I was finally putting myself first. Leaving the state seemed to be the only way to save me from being responsible for people who should no longer be my responsibility. It felt so freeing.

As I hung up the phone, my first thought was that *my mom must be blowing this out of proportion, as she tends to do.* X is my mellow child, super respectful, never in trouble, hard worker, kind-hearted, and very lovable. His hugs are powerful. His smile melts your heart, and his laughter gives you life. I've only been gone for four months! What could have possibly happened in such a short time? As overwhelming as it sounded, I knew I had to talk to him myself.

The next day as things continued to escalate in Minnesota, I finally got my son on the phone. I automatically heard the scattered conversation, random thoughts, comments that had nothing to do with what we were talking about, and extreme changes in emotions. My heart started pounding out of my chest; a deep sadness overtook my whole being. I felt overwhelmed beyond measure. As his mom, I knew this wasn't drugs. I knew this was mental. *Something is affecting my son's mind. What could it be, Lord? Why is this happening? What can I do about it? How will I be able to face this, whatever this is?*

As I hung up on him, because it was clear I wasn't speaking to *my* son, I knew there was no way I could do anything from another state. I knew I'd have to drop everything and move back to Minnesota to face whatever this was.

While I was breaking down internally, feeling like I had a 300-pound weight sitting on my chest, I asked my grandma can we talk? With sweaty palms and a dry throat, I said, "Grandma, I got some bad news about my job. They won't let me officially transfer my job here. I'm going to have to go back to Minnesota by next week." As I watched my grandma's shoulders droop and I saw the emptiness in her eyes from pure disappointment— my heart sank. I wasn't ready to share what was happening until I could embrace it myself. So I lied! I told them my job would not allow me to relocate to Denver officially. Not only was I trying to prepare my mind for what I'd be dealing with when it came to my son, but I was also trying to accept leaving my grandma. She helped raise me, and she needed me right now. So, with a heavy heart, I got ready for my departure.

As I drove what seemed to be the longest drive I've ever taken back to Minnesota, I dreaded what was ahead of me. *How will I be strong enough to face something so foreign to me? Why is this happening to my family, my son, and our life? I'm not equipped for something like this! I can't even process what's coming. Lord, please let your will be done!*

Back in Minnesota, as the entire house slept, I heard my son calling my name; he sounded uneasy, almost frightened. Hearing this noise in the middle of the night startled me out of my sleep. Before it woke anyone else up, I rushed down the stairs to see what was happening. I see X pacing back and forth in the kitchen, appearing agitated. "Mom, do you hear them calling for me? Uncle P is asking me to come outside. He is saying a bunch of shit. A couple of friends from school are out there too. They have the place surrounded; you hear them, right? What should I do, Mom? Should I just go out there?"

As he walked back and forth in the kitchen, holding his hands in a tight fist and breathing heavily, he was mumbling things to himself; it appeared he was talking to someone other than me. I looked into his glossed-over eyes, and it was as if he wasn't even there. His stare felt like he was looking through me; it felt intimidating. A darkness I'd never seen before came face to face with me that night. The person standing before me was not my son.

As my mind began to race, trying to make sure I said and did the right thing not to escalate the situation, it was as though I was having an out-of-body experience. In reality, I felt like fleeing. I can't handle any of this. I don't want to take any of this on. It was as though my body was shutting down from the inside out. My stomach was on fire, my chest felt like a vice grip was squeezing it, and my legs felt like noodles. I silently began to pray, *Father God, please fill this place with so many angels that Satan has no other option but to flee. Please, God, protect this household and my son from whatever this is and give me the strength to know what to do.* As I stood frozen in disbelief, I heard God whisper: *You have lived with a compulsive liar and sex addict for years, that is a form of mental illness, and you survived. You're stronger than you think. I've been preparing you for years, trust me!*

The next day I was forced to make one of the most complex decisions I've ever had to make as a mom. I had to either call the police to get my son some help or turn a blind eye to what was happening. Obviously, turning a blind eye is the easier decision. That way, you can be more like a friend instead of actually parenting. You can pretend you don't see what's in front of you instead of having to face it and do something about it. At that moment, I reminded myself that I was his mom! I was supposed to protect him no matter what. I had to fight my fears and do what was best for him. However, I was not only his mom; I was a black mom with a black son, which only heightened the fear of something going wrong.

What if they see him as a threat? What if I call the police to get my son the help he needs, but he loses his life in the hands of the police? No matter the fear I face, I have to lean on my faith by putting it in God's hands and making the call.

The battle was a roller coaster ride from there. There were many stressful days and many long nights. We went through cycles of him having various "episodes," calling the police, the ambulance coming, and talking him into going with them. Not to mention, of course, that he had to go "willingly" because they can't force an adult to go to the hospital, even one that appeared to be unstable. They may take him for a 72-hour hold (sometimes a few days longer), release him to anyone, even the streets, and then we'd be back to the beginning again.

Each time he was in the hospital, they couldn't trace anything in his system but marijuana. They told us it was difficult to identify what was going on with him unless his system was clean of toxins.

After a lot of push and pull, "we," (my mom, my brother, myself, and some powerful prayer warriors) fighting this battle head-on with my son, got him into an inpatient treatment center for drugs and alcohol. A few months into the program and completely sober, he had an "episode" in one of his group classes. He was seeing and hearing things; that didn't exist to anyone else in the classroom, which led to yet another hospital visit.

Doubtful that anything would change, but diligently praying it would, we finally got some answers!

The doctors determined after many tests and observations that he had schizoaffective disorder. They believe his illness occurred from smoking laced marijuana which changed his brain's chemical balance. On occasion, he would smoke marijuana and have a drink; however, once he started having "episodes" and would end up in the hospital, the only thing that showed up in his system was marijuana.

The doctors advised that some drugs are not traceable after so many hours of being in your system, so those would not show up in a test. They admitted that, unfortunately, they're seeing this happening to too many young adults within the past two years. People were coming in after smoking marijuana laced with some other drug, and their chemical balance was being changed, causing schizoaffective disorder and other mental health disorders.

It began to feel like a sense of relief; My son could now understand what was happening and have the guidance of professionals to understand what comes next and how to get things under control. My mom and I can finally take a deep breath, the doctors have it figured out, and they're now going to get him the help he needs to be successful. Wrong! With my son's illness, this is just the beginning of what's to come.

To afford the care required, you need to be low income or well off; the middle class won't due. I received a call that I needed to remove my son from the medical insurance I was receiving through my employer so that he could apply for medical insurance through the state. Removing him off my medical insurance would be the only way he could afford the prescriptions he'd have to be on for the rest of his life. It was also crucial for him to sign up for disability right away. He would need a team that included a social worker, psychiatrist, psychologist, case manager, doctors, and some family/friends willing to walk this journey with him for the rest of his life.

Unfortunately, the level of health care available to those with mental health-related diagnoses is not the same in every state. Most states have little to no programs or hospital support regarding mental health. Unfortunately, having schizoaffective disorder, like many mental health diseases, means being treated like a criminal instead of like someone with a health-related issue. When my son's battle started before being diagnosed, I had the opportunity to be blessed with a team of police officers that chose to become aware of who he was and what he was dealing with.

One of the officers pulled me aside and thanked me for fighting for my son the way I did. He told me to ensure he didn't fall into the criminal justice system, I'd need to continue to fight. He told me it was easier for the justice system to have him serve time than to continue going through the medical process. "Don't stop fighting for him; the system often fails those with mental health issues." I will forever be grateful to that officer for his honesty and care.

I realized all the things I thought I knew about mental health were judgments and assumptions with little to no facts. What you think you know about mental health, you don't. One doesn't honestly know until it touches your inner circle.

My son ended up on the streets at one time or going from shelter to shelter and in very unsafe situations he'd never intentionally put himself in. He has been removed from my home multiple times because of his "episodes." My son goes through times of not taking his medicine because of how it makes him feel, or he gets leveled out and feels he doesn't need them. My son has been judged or misled by family members who had no clue. My son struggles with accepting this diagnosis because he wasn't born this way and had a life full of work, friends, a girlfriend, and travel.

However, my son has also continued to hold down employment through it all. *My* son has continually fought to hold on through it all. It's *my* son who continues to fight for success through it all. It's *my* son, who just graduated from a carpentry program that took him 20 weeks to complete. It's *my* son who I will continue to fight for through it all. X will forever be *my* son! I have come to accept the darkness, rejoice in the glimpse of light and embrace my sons battle with mental health.

THE PRACTICE

"To find a glimpse of light in the darkest days, you have to find some healthy outlets and find hope in even the small wins."

~ Tanya Garner

Find a person/persons you can talk to about what's happening—someone you can trust that you can vent to. It's not always about them fixing it; sometimes, you just need someone to listen.

Find a local support group for parents with children battling mental health illness either through your city/state or through your church. I found a group through a church that met once a week at one of the member's homes. It included parents and those battling mental health. Even though my son wouldn't go, it was beneficial for my mom and me to attend.

Properly educate yourself on the diagnosis. It helps remove judgments and assumptions and prepares you for the truth. You want to deal with facts only; in an already confusing time.

Be a liaison for your child, no matter their age. Advocate for them, and be as involved as possible. It will help with getting the medical providers to take action. If your son or daughter is over age, medical providers won't talk to you or release information unless there is a signed release due to privacy laws, but you can give the medical providers information. Give them as much information as possible to assist with care or hospital holds.

Do not try to face this alone. You need a person if possible. Mine was my mom.

Over time, you'll find other people become involved based on who your son or daughter reaches out to. Educate them on signs to look for and how to handle certain situations, and remind them you're there to help. It helps you if others come to you before they react on assumption or their limited amount of knowledge.

Remember, every person and every situation is different—you can't handle it one way across the board. Your son or daughter may have the same diagnosis as someone else but handles things differently with some similarities. Keep track of who they are in those manic situations, their triggers, and how you know something isn't right.

Avoid telling everyone: Limit it to who needs to know or on a need-to-know basis; gossip, misdirection, and opinions (which everybody has) add stress you don't need.

Find a positive outlet that relaxes you (walking, running, yoga, hanging with friends). You'll need to find moments to relax, relate, and release.

Pray. Stand firm in your faith; you'll need it.

One of my favorite scriptures is Proverbs 3:5-6:

"Trust in the Lord with all your heart, and lean not on your own understanding; In all your ways acknowledge Him and He shall direct thy paths."

When we are no longer able to change a situation - we are challenged to change ourselves.

~ Viktor E. Frankl

Tanya Garner dedicates this chapter to her son X, who continues to amaze her with his strength through his battle with mental health, and to her mom, who walked this journey side by side with her as her "person" before losing her fight to pancreatic cancer. Tanya lives in Minnesota and is the loving mother of five children. Tanya spends most of her time raising her youngest amazing daughter, Aubri! Tanya also has one beautiful granddaughter, Nova, whom she loves spending time with. Tanya loves to dance and listen to music. Tanya uses music as a positive outlet to relax, relate, and release. Tanya is a true giver at heart. She loves to see others happy and succeeding and will do what she can to help them get there. Tanya is a woman of her word. She would rather be hurt with the truth than comforted with a lie. Tanya is a God-fearing woman that uses prayer for everything. Tanya hopes that her knowledge mixed with her experiences, can be a game changer in someone's life. Tanya is a published author. Tanya has a podcast with her sister Stephanie Bailey: Sisters on Love, Life, and Keeping it real!

Tanya would love for you to follow her on her social media pages.

If you would like to contact me regarding my knowledge about schizoaffective disorder see my information below:

Connect with Tanya:

Email: tbird101@icloud.com

Instagram: denvergirlmnworld

Facebook https://www.facebook.com/tanya.lmgarner

CHAPTER 20

A VISCERAL AWAKENING

HOW TO LET GO OF THE PAST TO IGNITE YOUR AUTHENTIC SELF

Georgia Wong, LAc., LMT

MY STORY

My worst fear was confirmed.

My mother told me I was a disappointment from the time of birth.

While staring at myself in the bathroom mirror, it slowly started happening again. The constriction of my throat, the tightness in my chest, the quickening of my heartbeat, it was all happening—again. The inability to take a full deep breath was overcoming my nervous system and sending me into more of a panic.

It's okay; you're okay, take a deep breath and hold it there, exhale, and get out of your fight or flight. Inhale. . .exhale. . .peace, love, joy, connection. . .inhale. . .exhale. Every tool for emotional training went into automatic mode.

Why does she always have the ability to do this to me with just her presence? You know you need to talk to her about the clearing, right? I thought to myself. *I mean, the whole reason you did the clearing was to create a better relationship with her. How were you supposed to know you would have that vision. The vision you would viscerally feel in every ounce of your being—the vision validating the story of not being enough and of being a disappointment. I need to get confirmation, and the only way is to ask her.*

"Mom, can we go for a walk?" I asked the petite Asian woman, sitting in the chair in the corner of our hotel room, reading from her iPad.

"Sure," she simply replied, "Let me finish getting ready, and we can go."

Great, I thought, *even more time to ruminate on what I need to ask.*

I could feel myself getting edgy. *It's okay; you're okay. Inhale. . .exhale.* I keep repeating the same phrase over and over, hoping it would stop the fear-based contracting thought from fully forming.

We finally made it outside the hotel in what seemed like an eternity, but it probably was more like 15 minutes. It was hot out. The Florida sun was high in the sky and beaming down in an impenetrable way. When combined with the rising humidity, and my equally rising anxiety, there was no mercy. A bead of sweat started forming on my brow. I could feel my clothes stick to my already moist skin.

"I need to talk to you about something," I said in the calmest voice I could muster. "I know this is going to sound a little woo-woo to you, but I did this thing called a clearing, where they tap into your subconscious to clear out any limiting beliefs no longer serving your greater self. I did it because I wanted to be able to create a better relationship with you." I explained. "I thought I could do this without sharing the experience with you, but something happened during the last part of the clearing, which was so disturbing."

My mother now was listening intently, so I continued, "I saw myself coming out of the birth canal. I felt safe and secure for one minute, then simultaneously felt something else. Something I had no idea how to describe. As I was getting closer and closer to the light at the end of the tunnel, the indescribable feeling started getting stronger and stronger. When I finally was in full vision, blinded by the bright light, I finally realized what the feeling was. It washed over me like a giant ocean wave. It hit every cell in my body; every ounce of my being was saturated with the feeling. It was the feeling of disappointment."

When I finished the story, I paused and looked at my mom. Now walking around the Legoland-covered parking lot, because it was the only shaded area we could find, she stopped walking.

"Is this true, Mom?" I asked, my voice shaking, holding back tears for what might be the answer. She was now looking down, although visibly not looking at anything. I could tell she was trying to come up with the right wording. There was a long pause—a pause that was deafening to my heart. *It's okay; you're okay. Inhale. . .exhale.*

"Georgia, I want to explain something to you," she started saying. "In our culture, it is important to have a boy to carry on the family name. When I had Becky, I knew I failed, and we would have to try again. I carried you differently. I didn't have the same symptoms I had when I was pregnant with Becky. Everyone thought you were going to be a boy. I mean, we didn't even have a girl's name picked out."

Oh shit. She's not denying it. I was a disappointment—a disappointment from the second I was born. I could feel my heart sinking.

"You came out, and you were a girl. I knew your father wasn't going to be happy," my mother said with sadness in her voice. "So, I can understand why you did feel like you were a disappointment. I think part of that is true," she confirmed.

WTF! This explains so much! I thought my head was going to explode. I suddenly had a flashback of every experience where I felt less than, not enough, insecure, etc.—all the times I tried to live up to being the "son" my father never had. I went fishing with him, picked worms and caught frogs for his lures, and he was tough and strong when I got hurt. "Stop crying!" he would scream, "You're fine!" I rode a BMX boy's bike he bought me while buying my sister a pretty pink girl's bike. I was the first child to go to work at our family-owned restaurant at the tender age of nine, not as a hostess or cashier like my sister, but as the dishwasher in the back, scrubbing pots and pans, lifting heavy bags of rice, sweeping and mopping the floor. It was all laid out in front of me. Even when, four years later, my brother Eric was born, the story was already imprinted on my soul. It was too late. My parents, of course, never openly discussed this point, but somehow it subconsciously got stuck into who I was becoming as a member of this family.

My father and my relationship were tumultuous, to say the least. We lived 45 minutes away from our family restaurant. Every night after closing, we fought all the way home, me sitting in the way back so he couldn't reach me. We screamed purgatives at each other, him becoming so enraged, calling me all the names: a brat, bitch, cunt; you get the idea. Me, thinking I could outsmart him by poking holes in all of his statements about how life is and what people expect from me. I ended up being a mirror image of everything my father didn't like about himself, yet he raised me to be exactly all of those things. I describe it as being a strong, independent, opinionated young woman with a can-do attitude. He described it as being a stubborn, rebellious, smart-ass, disrespectful child. Perspectives make all the difference—more on this a little later.

Experiences to solidify the already formed thought of not being enough started showing up. Everything from being teased with racial slurs for being one of the three Asian kids at school (the other two were my siblings) to having my mom disappointed in me receiving an A-, versus all As.

It also showed up in my continuous journey to figure out who I was and what I wanted to do when I grew up. My life became an endless pursuit of careers. This part of my journey is a mixture of circumstance meets curiosity meets opportunity. Due to the violent physical and verbal abuse my father used to discipline me and my inability to be a quiet, obedient girl, his thoughts were very clear about my education after high school.

"You can either stay in this house so I can watch your every move, or you find your own way," my father screamed in yet another rageful fight between us. "I'm not going to waste my hard-earned money (on you) otherwise."

Point taken, I thought to myself, *I don't want anything from you anyway, asshole.* I then promptly drove myself down to the Army recruiter's office and signed up for eight years in the military. What was ironic about this event was when I did it, I wasn't yet 18 years old and legally responsible for myself, so the recruiter had to go down to our restaurant and have my parents sign me away. At that moment, I thought they were signing my freedom papers. I knew I finally escaped another beating physically or verbally from ever happening again.

Eight years in the service led to 20-year retirement, including three military occupations and one deployment for Iraqi freedom. I vividly remember being in basic training at Ft. Jackson, South Carolina, and realizing I was thousands of miles from my hometown. I was surrounded by girls of all ethnicities and walks of life. I also quickly grasped I was alone without guidance from my family or friends back home, and I needed to figure out what I stood for without them. It was the beginning of truly finding my authentic self.

I ended up getting a cosmetology license, a massage license, becoming certified to teach yoga, a bachelor's in science in nutrition-dietetics and integrative therapy practices, endless certificates for different modalities in bodywork, and a master's degree in acupuncture. Sprinkle in training for endurance races, getting married, having a son, and owning and running my own business, all through a global pandemic, and you have the life of someone trying to prove their worth through accomplishment. Reflecting on all the years I was in school; I realized that, as grateful as I was to have all the degrees and knowledge under my belt, I was pushed by one common theme, one common denominator—the theme of not being enough. I had the feeling of having to prove myself over and over, yet whenever I finished with another degree or another accomplishment, I still felt anxious and empty. And worse yet, I was exhausted. I knew at that moment it was time to make a change.

There have been a few a-ha moments in my life. Advice on giving myself space and grace, not being so hard on myself, and understanding that everyone has freedom of choice and self-evolution are all things I had to learn the hard way. I believe every soul is to learn a lesson while we're here on Earth. Whether or not you choose to see the signs surrounding you on what you should do for your next step is up to you. It's about paying attention and listening—listening to your soul and your unique vision and intuition. Your soul will tell you what you need to do. It takes bravery to do it. This is why a lot of people choose not to do it. For many, it's easier to know what the day-to-day is than to step out of the box and be uncomfortable. What's so amazing is that once out of that box and into the uncomfortable, something happens. It's called growth. We're all here to grow.

Part of growing is learning to let go of things no longer serving us. However, the phrase "letting go" has always stumped me. Even in traditional Chinese medicine (TCM), the organ responsible for letting go of grief, sadness, etc., is the large intestine. It seems fitting when knowing the function of the large intestine is excretion, but I digress. We as a society say it so easily, but if it was so easy to accomplish, then why would it be such a big deal? Frankly, it's because it's not easy. No one knows how to let go automatically. And let me tell you, letting go doesn't require forgiveness of someone else; it's about finding forgiveness with yourself. It takes self-reflection and truly knowing and trusting your unique belief system to understand how to let go. Maybe it's not even a matter of letting go but a redefinition of the terms of your agreement to how your treat yourself. Hopefully, it's with space and grace and, ultimately, love.

The following is how I found peace with my past and how I unpacked all the layers of beliefs set upon me while growing up. This is how I finally discovered my authentic self at age 47 and no longer need the stories to push me into proving them wrong. Maybe it'll help you. Maybe it will get you started on a journey of self-discovery and reflection. Just know that change is possible with these tools.

THE PRACTICE

As a holistic practitioner, I would be doing a disservice by not stressing how important the basics of health relate to overall well-being. The basics are restful sleep, eating a nutrient-dense whole food diet to create a healthy microbiome, and daily exercise to move your Qi (vital energy) and blood. However, your mind is a powerful tool where you can begin to overcome all of the myths you've been telling yourself thus far. I know making this change might sound insurmountable, but trust yourself. You deserve this.

Define Your Vision: Setting your vision is one of the first steps in being able to let go of the stories no longer serving you. You need to know where you're headed in order to make the choices that'll get you there. Ask yourself where emotionally you would like to be. Is it joy, peace, abundance? Shoot for the stars with your vision. Even if you don't hit the target straight away, it will land you much further than what you originally ever thought was possible.

Becoming Clear About Your Emotional Patterns: The key takeaway from this chapter is how *emotion* drives *outcomes*. It doesn't happen any other way. Once you have emotional resilience and can create from a love-based state, the energy will overflow into other parts of your life, whether it's your relationships, career, or health. It will shift.

What emotional state do you reside in the most? Most likely, it's only a few. Anger, anxiety, and frustration are all fear-based contracting states. It generally sends you into rumination of thought. It doesn't serve your greater self to stay in this state, for it doesn't allow you to expand and get to your vision. Plus, staying in these thought patterns strengthens their existence, making them easier to get to whenever triggered. Create a new pattern, and work on strengthening it. Checking in with yourself every hour or two and simply asking yourself how you feel will tell you if your comfort zone is a more fear-based contacting state or a love-based expanding state. Just an FYI, neither too much of either one is a great thing to be in all the time. For example, in TCM, being too joyous or happy leads to being manic. There needs to be a balance of yin and yang (pronounced yong).

Breathe Your Way into a New Neuro Pathway: Once you figure out your emotional patterns, it's time to do the work of changing them. It's done through meditation and box breathing; a four-count inhale, a four-count pause at the top of the inhale, and an eight-count exhale. It's used to take yourself out of your amygdala, where the sympathetic fight and flight responses occur in your brain. It is most useful when those fear-based thoughts are triggered and you need a tool to quickly get you out of fight or flight. Being able to use the breath to connect our mind and heart space is invaluable. However, when first beginning to meditate, be nice to yourself. It might take several times to be able to meditate into a place of calmness. Even when you've been doing it for years, it can be hard to get into the zone. Don't judge it but keep at it. Consistency is key.

Connecting the New Emotional Pattern: Remember that vision I told you to identify? It's now time to connect the vision to the breath. When doing your meditation, acknowledge how you feel, don't judge it, and don't give it power one way or the other. Think of your vision and state why you deserve that emotion. For example, I am at peace because I can be. Simple, easy. Don't make this step hard. Repeat this over and over. Sit with it. Associate a time when you have felt your emotional vision in your life, so every cell, every essence of your being, believes it's already happening.

You will notice the more you put in the work (the meditation, breathwork, feeling your vision), the less you will feel (input fear-based state here).

Create a Mantra and Scream it from the Rooftop: Do it even if you feel silly. Stand in the stance which best displays the emotion. Say it whenever you start having self-doubt. For example, mine was, "I'm a badass bitch." It could take on tons of meaning, but it instantly brought empowerment to my soul. It made me feel like I could conquer anything. Find one that fits your soul and do it. Period.

Always Reflect and Evaluate:

Experiences in life are a blessing.

Perspective on those experiences are game-changers in how you respond to life. Emotions will drive these responses, and it's important to use your frontal cortex, not your amygdala, to make thoughtful decisions about your life. Sometimes being in those uncomfortable transition times is necessary to access the passageway to the other side of knowing yourself better. However, being able to listen to your heart's song and peeling off those layers to uncover the best version of you is worth all the work it takes to get there. With love and light, show up for yourself because you're worth it.

Georgia, a first-generation Asian American, was born as a middle child in Duluth, Minnesota. She began her journey in the healing arts in Minneapolis, Minnesota, upon returning from active duty in the US Army, where she graduated from the Minneapolis School of Massage and Bodywork in 2002. A lifelong learner, she surrounds herself with understanding the belief in the body's ability to heal itself. She uses all the tools she has learned over her life, helping to facilitate and restore health and wholeness to the body. She is a strong believer in being proactive about taking care of your body.

She enjoyed her successful practice in Minneapolis before relocating to Colorado to continue her education in attaining her bachelor of science in nutrition and integrative therapy practices, where her goal is to help give knowledge to people, so they are empowered to choose the right method of healing for themselves. She restarted her practice, Breathe Energy Bodywork, in 2013, got married, and had a beautiful baby son before heading back once again to complete her master's in acupuncture.

Georgia's philosophy is to look at the person holistically, addressing all areas of the body to bring back balance while reducing stress and tension. She creatively combines a mixture of massage, nutrition, and Traditional Chinese Medicine modalities to tailor to each of her client's individual needs.

When she is away from working with clients, Georgia loves being active, whether it's playing with her son, taking a yoga class, taking a HIIT class, or hiking a mountain. She loves deep talks with loved ones, connection through amazing healthy food, and traveling.

Connect with Georgia:

Instagram: breatheenergy

Website: www.breatheenergybodywork.com

CHAPTER 21

WE ARE NEVER TRULY LOST

HOW LIFE'S CHALLENGES CAN MAKE US QUESTION OUR FAITH

Jennifer Tasker

MY STORY

Life can get hard and messy sometimes, but it can also be humbling, raw, and beautiful. The best part is that we are all so much stronger than we give ourselves credit for, and when given a chance, you can live the happy life you deserve.

I was a lively and talkative 70s indigo child who loved to make everyone smile and laugh with my silly songs and playful ways. I was a psychic dreamer, often scaring my family with my accuracy and ability to see and hear Spirit. As odd as some of those around me thought I was, it was through this trusted connection with Spirit that I was able to make it through some very difficult challenges, even though my faith continued to be tested time and again.

I became an adult at five years old, thanks to a neighborhood teenager who robbed me of my innocence.

This incredibly traumatic experience not only taught me things I had no right to know at such a young age but naturally plagued me with self-love issues, questioning every change my body went through. Thankfully, whenever I felt lost or confused, Spirit would show up and guide me back to my light—forever urging me to let it go, find a way to move forward, and focus on what was in front of me. You would usually find me singing, having grown up in a very musical family. I enjoyed the best of every single day and always looked forward to spending time outside with nature, where I felt most at home, sometimes with my head in the clouds but always listening.

Throughout my grade school years, I was bullied every day. "Look at that wild-looking, red-haired, freckle-faced weirdo!" Were the words often accompanied by a shove or a kick.

This did not help to improve my self-love issues, and to top it all off, I had a lot of health struggles. As a coping mechanism, I began writing poems, many beyond the wisdom of my birth years, and I became obsessed with running and soccer. I was pretty darn good and quite fast, so I put everything I had into it. Anything to be the best at something and make the other kids like me. It seemed the better I got, the harder things became. *Why am I always being tested?* Nothing seemed to make them like me, and it got more and more difficult for me to keep my chin up and rise above it all. I did my best to listen to Spirit and remain optimistic that things would eventually get easier.

In my 15th year, I had a particularly bad day. One of those days where it felt like everything that could possibly go wrong—did. To top it all off, I had another migraine. I felt nauseous as my head began to pound; I could feel my body begin to shake as I rummaged through the bathroom cabinet for the aspirin bottle. Frustrated and in pain, I staggered back to my room, stopping myself from slamming the door. *Mom is sleeping.* Quietly I closed the door and melted into a puddle on the floor, feeling completely deflated. Screaming inside, *Why does this keep happening to me? What is wrong with me? I can't do this anymore. I need it to stop.* I need to make it all stop. As the tears fell down my face, my thoughts were spiraling as I was mindlessly taking pill after pill, clearly far too many for a headache. I heard the word "Stop!" in my head so loudly that I was physically startled and found myself staring in shock at what was left of the pills scattered on the floor beside me. Aware of the enormity of what I was doing, I was overcome with the urge to call for my mom. "Mom!" "Mom, I need your help!" I can only imagine how she must have felt seeing me on the floor like that.

Thankfully before it was too late, my mom got me the help I needed, and I'm here to share my story with you. As scary as it was, I am so glad I called out to her and was brave enough to share how sad and overwhelmed I felt instead of keeping it bottled up inside. To this day, she remains my closest confidant and one of the brightest lights in my life. She found me a wonderful therapist where I learned to talk about how I felt and how to shift my focus back onto being my best self for me, not the approval of others.

At just 17, I was diagnosed with very painful Stage 4 Endometriosis, and to add to the shock factor, the doctor just looked at me and said point-blank, "Jennifer, I am afraid you won't be able to have any children. Things are a real mess in there, and it would be much too dangerous for you to carry a child." My ears began to roar, and I felt the blood drain from my face. I heard myself saying, *Sorry, what?* I'm not sure if it was in my head or out loud because the doctor just kept right on talking, something about surgery and other options, but it was all too much for me to hear; I would never have any children.

I always wanted a family the size of the Von Trapps. Hearing this news felt like my heart shattered into a million little pieces. *I just can't believe it. They must be wrong; they have to be.* Later that very night, Spirit came to me in a dream as my grandfather on my mother's side. He said, *You are an old soul and have lived many lives. You have a very important mission to accomplish and only ten years to do so. It's going to be difficult, and there will be times you'll want to give up, but you have what you need inside you to follow through.* The only real hint he gave me as to what this all meant was a name, Joshua.

Not even a year later, I met my husband and soul mate.

We've had an amazing time growing, learning, and making mistakes together. We both wanted a family of our own, and I was now convinced that my grandfather meant the doctors were wrong and I was to have a son. Grandpa was right; it was a very long hard road. I had 26 surgeries and 17 miscarriages over the next nine years. We endured great loss but were blessed with two beautiful children only a few years apart. My daughter Janelle—my miracle—arrived first, and only a few years later came the infamous Joshua. They are incredibly brilliant and inspiring lights. Whenever I am with them, my heart wants to burst, it's so full! They truly are my happy place. Thank goodness we never gave up on them being in our life. Ten years after the visit from my grandfather, I had my 27th surgery, a total hysterectomy. As a result, I was gifted the first pain-free year of my life.

Thirteen months later, I came down with a very strange case of hives.

I took some antihistamines and waited it out, but I just kept getting worse. I focused all the light and faith I could muster on this mysterious reaction which did help to calm my mind, but it did not seem to help these itchy and painful red bumps that were beginning to cover my entire body. Here I was days later, getting much worse and having all sorts of scary symptoms. I was at my desk at work speaking with one of our residents when I started to have a tickle in my throat that quickly turned into trouble breathing. I was rushed to the emergency room head to toe in hives and full-blown anaphylaxis—the cause: Unknown.

After three grueling years of emergency room visits and a confusing whirlwind of specialists, I was put on total disability with a diagnosis of Mast Cell Activation Syndrome, a form of Mastocytosis—an exceedingly rare hereditary condition that causes my body to produce way too many mast cells. Our mast cells are there to protect and alert our body to a variety of dangers and allergens and work to protect us from said danger. However, in a condition like mine, with just too many overactive mast cells, my body is on constant high alert and always in what we call a "flare" just beneath the surface. Due to the unpredictable and sensitive nature of this condition, almost anything can trigger me and cause me to go into anaphylactic shock. There is no cure, and the recommended medications cause many other unpleasant sensitivities, are often dangerous, and offer limited relief.

I was terrified and validated at the same time hearing this news. I felt an odd sense of relief, but the first thought that went through my head was, *Am I going to die?* I was glad I finally had a name to put to it, but to say that there is no cure and that my future looked dim was unacceptable to me. I became virtually obsessed with finding a cure—frantically scouring the internet using every resource I could think of, but the rarity of this condition had me hitting roadblock after roadblock. My heart was racing with worry that I had passed this scary disease onto my children, whom we fought so hard for. This made me question everything I believed. I somehow convinced myself that my light was being used against me, and eventually, I became consumed by the condition itself. I became my illness.

I lost my ability to depend on myself. I even lost faith in my connection with Spirit, something I came to rely on with my entire being. On an especially hard day, I found myself howling at the moon like an angry wolf, "Where are you now? How much can one soul endure? Why are you not here when I need you the most?" The lack of response left me feeling deflated and lost. I withdrew from all my friends and family, from life itself, and my light dimmed.

I spent days in bed, unable to move my body, depressed, anxious all the time, and terrified to leave my own home in fear of a flare. This continual focus on my fears and negativity caused them to grow, and then it finally happened. I went into a horrible flare I couldn't get out of. I later learned I was so sick by this point that I should have died. I remember lying in my bed, and everything started to go dark and fuzzy.

I don't remember going to the emergency room.

The smell of alcohol tickled my nose, and I could hear alarms beeping and the whispers of the people rushing around me, but I wasn't able to make out their words. I heard a young baby crying, and I remember thinking: *That precious little life must be so scared.* Suddenly the beeping got very loud, and there were shouts. Then it became so bright I couldn't see anything except this vibrant glow. I was overcome with the most glorious and beautiful light-filled feeling. It was greater and more powerful than I had ever experienced in my life before. I thought this was the end of this journey for me. I was crossing over.

I remember feeling so warm and calm, like I was being bathed in love. I felt a hand on my heart, and I could hear a woman's voice: "You're okay now, dear. You are not alone." I felt overcome with joy and gratitude for being alive, for the very miracle of my existence. *Spirit reminded me that with the acceptance of myself and my circumstances, I'm growing and strengthening my soul's path. I need to allow my doubts, fears, and insecurities to flow through but not reside in me. It's okay for me to be sad sometimes and to make mistakes, as long as I remember to learn and grow from them, or else I will stay stuck cycling, barely existing, and that's not what I'm here for. I'm meant to love and embrace my lightness and share it with the world.*

I felt complete again. Spirit was there all this time; my light was never really lost; I just forgot to listen.

Sitting here on a warm summer evening several years after this life-altering day, I feel so blessed for all these gifts I've been given.

From the years of abuse and bullying, I was gifted forgiveness and the beautiful purity of self-love. From the years of pain, I was gifted with tolerance, endurance, and perseverance. Today, living with mast cell disease is a challenging journey. You never know what you're going to get each day, as the symptoms and effects are always changing and adapting. Befriending those tricky little cells has gifted me the ability to embrace and make the most of each-and-every moment.

As I journey in and out of flares alternating the good days and the bad, I feel almost as if I'm waxing and waning like the moon. I do my best to focus on the blessings in each day I'm gifted and remind myself that my powerful light will always show me the way. I'm so grateful to be home with my family, and for the days I'm able to write and share some inspiration, laughter, or thought-provoking quote. I'm even thankful for those bad days, the resting times, as they always make me feel lighter and stronger, getting brighter with each flare I overcome. In these moments, I feel like I'm literally glowing in all my light, giving me the courage, and strength I need, to continue to persevere and move through and beyond this recent challenge.

Life is always going to be full of storms. This is our journey. How we choose to maneuver through them so we can bask in the sun is our destiny.

THE PRACTICE

THREE WAYS TO HELP REKINDLE YOUR GRATITUDE FOR LIFE

AWAKENING WITH PRESENCE

When you take the time to ponder who you really are, you realize you really are a miracle.

When you first awaken, gift yourself a few minutes to check-in. Find appreciation in the gifts offered to you in this moment, such as the miracle of your breath moving through your lungs or the feeling of your head on your soft pillow. Enhance your self-awareness by beginning your day focusing on the miracle that is you and the blessing that is the present. This practice reduces stress, increases feelings of joy, serenity, and peace, and can set the tone for your day.

WORK ON LETTING IT FLOW

Life doesn't always go as planned, but thankfully like the sun, we awaken with the chance to begin again.

If you're feeling out of sorts, go outside for a moment and look around; notice the birds flying freely and singing a tune. Life is in full bloom all around you, ever-moving, ever-changing. Nature is constantly adapting to its environment. Like how a tree just bends and flows with the wind as it bathes in the rain, washing away any dust or debris, and when the storm passes and the sun breaks through the clouds, the tree will gently shed the rain away, basking in and reaching for the light, growing taller and stronger with each new storm. This reminds you that all things can and will constantly adapt to their environment in their own unique time.

MAINTAINING BALANCE WITH MINDFULNESS

Stop worrying about the things you cannot control. Be mindful of your moments, as they won't be repeated.

Our light source is a whisperer continuously sending us loving, positive, forward-moving, and problem-solving thoughts. The closer you listen, the further you travel towards who you truly are! Being mindful of the signals your body is giving you can be immensely powerful.

If you're feeling overwhelmed, try asking yourself these three questions:

"How do I feel about this situation?"

"Will this serve my purpose?"

"What should I do?"

The key step that many of us forget is to quietly wait for the answers to come, and they will. Often this is felt in your core (tummy) before it reaches your brain, and basically, you'll feel the answer. We're a complicated and amazing species indeed.

Being mindful means to slow right down and be aware of your breath, your movements, and your very being. Find the volume button on your light source and turn it up full blast! Learn to depend on this voice as if it were your closest ally because, trust me, it is! The more mindful and aware of this voice you become, the more enlightened and filled with love you will feel. You'll begin to live and breathe love, become mindful of all the glorious moments, and you'll love all of them, the good and the bad.

Jennifer Tasker

Jennifer Tasker is an empath, light energy worker, and clairvoyant. Her intuitive and inventive nature, coupled with her boundless optimism, allows her to see solutions and opportunities that others may have overlooked. Her passions include writing, spending time with nature, and uplifting and empowering others to live their best lives despite their obstacles. A treasured resource for The Wellness Universe, Jennifer is a positive inspiration and truly represents all she shares with the world. She approaches every day with authentic, heart-based energy that allows everyone to always feel heard, seen, and supported. For Jennifer, every day is a gift!

Connect with Jennifer:

The Wellness Universe
https://www.thewellnessuniverse.com/world-changers/jennifertasker

Facebook
https://www.facebook.com/bepositivewithjennytasker

Instagram
https://www.instagram.com/jennydtasker/

CHAPTER 22

READY OR NOT, HEAR I COME

RISING ABOVE YOUR COMFORT ZONE FOR AN INCREDIBLE LIFE

Lori Frisher, CEO of Ready or Not! Media

MY STORY

Imagine your elementary school principal tells your mother you're going to be a "problem child." He gives up on you before you even graduate elementary school. Then to learn your mom was in a car accident shortly after she receives upsetting news from your principal. Your mom is your everything, your best friend! When she hurts, you hurt.

Or better yet you're in your first semester of college, sitting in class, with 300-plus freshman students, not knowing a soul, trying to follow the curriculum, homesick, sitting on uncomfortable auditorium chairs, wondering how you're going to make it through college the next four years.

There's nothing but silence. You can't hear what the professor is saying, so you suffer through the semester in an absolute daze, too insecure to use your voice and bring attention to the fact that you're different from the classmates.

Ready or not, it was time I had to spread my wings. I had butterflies in my stomach the night before giving the charge to my graduating class.

I looked with uncertainty out to all the empty white chairs on the school lawn thinking: *What did I get myself into?* I looked at my father and he pointed to his eye. Eye of the Tiger was our signal to fight through my fears and come out stronger.

I became the school's first student-elected commencement speaker with a disability. I was blessed to have the opportunity to speak publicly in front of 8,000 people for the first time in my life about my journey as a student with a disability, a division 1 athlete, and a member of a sorority.

After graduation I used my creativity to work around my disability and launched an advertising, enterprise sales, and marketing career. I'm not a big fan of corporate America and always had an entrepreneurial itch.

Accomplished as I was, I always tried to be a perfectionist. I dressed in stylish, fashionable high heels walking through the streets of New York City and set my hair in pink Velcro rollers before painting the town red. I had a calendar behind my door where I wrote down what I wore each day, so I wouldn't repeat outfits—so tiring. My thick, natural red hair was the attention getter and I thought if I looked hip and cool, I'd be accepted, and my disability would be overlooked by others. Or sometimes even me. That wasn't always the case. My hearing loss was there with me and I did my best every day. When I was younger I hid it. With age and life experiences I learned this is who I am, and I'm proud of it.

Imagine, counting down the minutes to dash through the exit door at your local boutique hair salon, staring into the oversized silver mirror in front of you. You cannot hear the hairdresser speaking to you. You nod yes to everything people say because all you want to do is act like you heard what was discussed. Tears start to well up fast as you notice your hair is four inches shorter after the stylist said he would cut two.

I was the first candidate in the world to use an invisible hearing device with a cochlear implant which gifted me new sounds. It was an honor to be gifted this life-changing device! I shared the superhuman story with others to help them believe that ground-breaking technology existed, and that it could transform your life. A camera crew followed me for nine weeks until the miraculous device was turned on.

Hearing water while shampooing my thick red hair under the faucet was truly incredible. To learn the sound of my sweet Pomeranian panting in the elevator for the first time! Wow, no more moments of car passengers repeating "You might want to turn your blinker off." It was amazing to hear the blinker! To be able to hear the tennis ball hitting the racquet after my doubles partner in high school, Christine, was the ears I didn't have. She gave me a thumbs up to show the ball was in, and if not in, a thumbs down. She always pumped me up on the court. I loved her energy and knew it was contagious. We both knew the importance of spreading good energy.

Everyone needs a cheerleader and to be given a compliment every now and then, for sure. She meant more to me than she knew. Spreading that good energy to others has been something I try to do at least once a day. Inspiring others to believe in themselves makes me smile.

Standing on the subway platform waiting for the N train after getting caught in the torrential downpour in rush hour, my pinstripe, navy Tahari pants suit was completely drenched, sticking to my legs. I quickly threw my frizzy hair up in a clip. A beautiful tall brunette woman, mid 30s taps my shoulder to tell me her young daughter standing at the end of the platform noticed I wore hearing aids.

She said, "Mommy I want to go home to put my hearing aids on. That lady is so cool!" I told the young girl she was very pretty and heard that she wears hearing aids like me. She says, "Mine are home and when I get off the train I'm putting them on." We both hugged tight. I shared with her mom, "It took me a long time to wear my hair up, but it's moments like this that inspire me to be me!"

It's great to give back, it doesn't need to be in monetary gifts; I've learned words can be gifts! Words can be powerful, used to inspire, motivate, make one feel valued.

Talk about a gift. One unforgettable summer night on the west side of Manhattan outside this trendy cafe, I ran into Michael Bolton, one of my absolute favorite musicians, who was leaning up against car parked along the sidewalk.

"Hi Michael."

"Do I know you?"

"Now you will. I know you hear this a lot. I am your biggest fan. Hard of hearing since I was three years old. You are one of my favorite musicians. I can listen, understand, and hear your music at the same time."

He then says, "Can I give you a hug, that is the nicest compliment I have ever heard."

You never know how far a hug can go. When I was diagnosed with stage 3 skin cancer, not once but twice, I appreciated all the hugs I could get to fight through it. There were intense moments where I didn't know if I'd come through, but prayer and love from strangers and family made me see the hope.

I'm not a fan of hospitals! *Who is?* It triggers me from when I was sick. The time was around 8 p.m. when I went to the ER during the COVID pandemic, not a place you want to be. My level of exhaustion was intense, I had severe muscle aches with serious hand tremors, my breathing was labored, I had brain fog, and I felt like I had a dozen bricks on my chest.

I felt even worse when I had an extremely hard time understanding the receptionist who wore a surgical mask. She showed signs of frustration banging her clipboard on desk. I'm sure she didn't want to be there given the heightened spread of the virus.

A security guard witnessed my struggle when I arrived at the ER. I was on the verge of tears while handing over my insurance ID. I felt like absolute crap. Praying the admin wouldn't ask for anything else, all I wanted to do was to go to sleep and feel better. The emergency doctor came out wearing his surgery mask and I couldn't make out anything he was saying either. Feeling sicker by the minute, tears fall as I know I now must repeat myself to the medical team that I'm deaf. Under my breath, I mumbled to myself, "I'm so tired of this!"

"Doctor, can we please FaceTime my family so they can interpret the visit tonight for me?" The doctor made an eye roll, like I was bothering him.

His irritability reminded me of a few years ago when the dentist pulled my tooth out of left field and the Novocain didn't work. I thought about that stupid mask he wore and me nodding, thinking he said something different. There was so much pain! The doctor said, "I told you I was going to pull the tooth." Certainly, I would've asked him for more novocaine. Obviously, I didn't hear him. *Thank goodness I only see the dentist one or two times a year. Keep flossing, brushing my teeth and have less Sour Patch Kids.*

I'm grateful to many doctors, but wonder if they like what they do. I also wonder if they are overworked. On a positive note, during my final surgery during the pandemic a nurse used sign language while wearing the see-through mask when checking in.

Whether it was doctors, or other men in my life, those relationships seemed more challenging than with women. I felt calmer around women.

I used to catch myself second guessing men. Men, more than women, make me feel small sometimes. Most of the time, I notice women who come in my path are more empathetic and understanding. I also learned when being authentic with men as I have gotten older I feel more at peace.

I was a tomboy growing up, was better in sports than most of the boys. But always questioned why teenage boys were so mean. Why are they laughing in my face to the point where I feel the spit from their big mouths? Imitating my lisp? Nonstop giggling during recess. "You talk funny! You have an accent! Do you wear a retainer?" I thought this would be the last time I'd hear these immature comments but unfortunately history repeated itself in my mid 30s as I was coming home from a party.

"Ma'am, do you know you were speeding?"

"Yes, sorry, it's dark, not familiar with road and wanted to catch up to my friend."

"Have you been drinking?"

"Yes, one drink over five and a half hours ago."

Shining his flashlight onto my face, "Open your mouth!" I panic and don't understand why I must open my mouth.

"You are talking funny. Sounds like you have something in your mouth. I said, open your mouth! Ma'am, please get out of the vehicle." I felt like I was drowning.

I asked him to move into the light from the headlights to read his lips. I was trembling from the cold aside from being nervous that I was being interrogated and felt like I would get arrested for standing up for myself.

I walked a straight line and passed the breath analyzer test. No ticket but the officer gave me his card to go out. Yes, to go out with him! I ignored him. He led me to Highway 36 and I immediately threw out his business card when I arrived home. This felt like the longest drive; I was nauseous and so hurt by the officer's interrogation. It left such a bad taste in my mouth, how powerless I felt with a man.

These questions have come up: *Do I trust men? Am I afraid he'll find out I'm not as perfect as he thought I was? Am I more insecure than he thinks? Will he like me even if I have flaws?*

Mr. Good-Looking reads into my puzzled face to reassure me all is good. My cochlear implant just fell off my head into the car cup holder while in the heat of the moment. It doesn't faze him. Me, on the other hand, the scene repeatedly plays in my head, thinking he's going to lose interest in me because of my hearing loss. I feel like I'm in quicksand. Relationships can be scary, and yet, can be beautiful.

Am I supposed to be married by the age of 28? Or marry a man of my faith? What will my friends and parents say if I date an older man? Am I supposed to please my family or myself? What is it like to date a woman? Is it possible I could love a man and a woman? What does that look like?

Yes, all of it was possible. I dated younger and older men, laughed and cried, and was with a woman for five years. I hid it from my family for a while but at the end of the day, all everyone wanted for me was to be happy. I explained that for me it wasn't about the gender; it was all about the heart. All I wanted was to feel loved, and still do.

This was a different relationship, and a time I had to be true to myself. I was ready to go out in public with a woman as my girlfriend. We were friends, she was beautiful, great smile, loved dogs, treated people the way I wanted to be treated. It gave me permission to love from my heart to hers and from her heart to mine.

She showed her love to me in ways I never received both physically and emotionally. In many ways, she allowed me to be vulnerable with her. We were similar in how we put others first before ourselves.

I thought about what a relationship was supposed to be. No relationship is perfect. You learn lessons. I wanted my partner to believe in me, and vice versa. I wanted a cheerleader, lover, protector, one who was smart, someone who was affectionate, a supporter, and someone who could make me laugh. Finally, I was getting comfortable in my own skin.

After many years of hiding my disability in relationships, I shared with my partner, "I don't hear at night once my devices are removed." The best memory was when I finger spelled in my partner's hand, signing, "I love you." This brought comfort, and we ended the day feeling loved.

I love to love. Yes, love hurts but I can honestly say through each relationship I have learned love lessons. I have been blessed to all those who have come into my life.

Today, I continue to navigate who will be the love of my life. I look forward to the journey and say this with such a smile on my face.

Another relationship I had gave me ten good years. It was my Esteem hearing device. It was time to move on and upward. My device battery life had terminated and I had to make a big decision whether I would wear two cochlear implants or go in another direction?

In 2020, I came to terms about my future: being deaf in both ears. I was ready to find a partnership that would bring me new miracles. My new life would be with two cochlear implants. They are my best friends. They go wherever I go. They have made me rise above my comfort zone to live an incredible life through my work and my community. Most importantly, they've have made me be more authentic in loving myself and sharing that love. Imagine that!

I've learned to live my best life. I never had to imagine any of this, because this is the life of me, Lori Frisher. This was and is my reality and therefore is no escaping it.

Today, I lead with my heart and accept this journey of who I am and know the adversity and gifts in my life have made me passionate about sharing with others. Ready or not, hear I come!

THE PRACTICE

We learn it's true: without our health we have nothing. Clearing our head isn't always easy. Have you ever felt like your head is ready to explode? How do I bring myself into the present to get centered? How do I be kind to me? What is it I need to focus on?

Any Rocky fans here? They call me a fighter! My song is, *Eye of the Tiger.* If you have a song that pumps you up, turn it up! Not only did I battle hearing loss since a toddler, but I am a two-time skin cancer survivor and was diagnosed in late 2020 with a functional neurological disorder. I had to start making healthy mental and physical decisions to improve my life. These trials and tribulations empower me and I'm confident they can do the same for you.

1. **Start Each Day with Gratitude**

   Say, "Thank you for this day!" Have a morning routine and dive into what you're grateful for. Repeat affirmations about abundance, prosperity, wealth, and success to kick the day off. Play uplifting songs that bring on a positive mindset.

2. **Move Your Body**

   Time for the gym: Shift your mindset, put your phone on silent, cue up the pre-programed songs and podcasts, refrain from all calls, texts, and emails until after your workout. Focus on the task. Listening to the beat of songs will trigger beautiful flashbacks from your younger years of where you were and who you were with when that song was playing.

3. **Surround Yourself with Positive People/Drama-Free Situations**

   Spend quality time with those that make you smile. Give yourself permission to take care of you first. Call or text someone to let them know you're thinking of them. Compliment a stranger. Let negativity out of your space. Create healthier boundaries.

4. **Like-Minded People**

   Like-minded people bring the best out in you. Your most creative ideas come, and you're at your best when you're in the presence of quality people.

5. **Be Present**

   Focus on those in front of you. Keep the blue light away; remember, the phone sleeps when you sleep. Your dreams will be sweeter.

6. **Immerse In Nature**

   Keep the body moving, breathe in all that surrounds you and you will start noticing new things, colors, trees, smells of flowers, the dew on grass. Life is brighter when you focus on your surroundings.

Lori Frisher, is a leader, entrepreneur, advocate, athlete, survivor, and public speaker who dares to dream beyond present circumstances to what is possible. Born with severe hearing loss, she spent 30-plus years relying on hearing aids, and competed at varsity levels in sports, although she was unable to hear any audible signals. At the University of Hartford, she earned a spot on the Division 1 tennis team as a walk-on, along with both academic and athletic scholarships. Lori continued to excel beyond her disability, along with overcoming Stage 3 cancer twice.

In 2010, a new, groundbreaking technology opened the world of sound for Lori. The first FDA-approved fully implantable hearing device alleviated Lori's sensorineural hearing loss. For the first time she was able to hear the sounds the rest of the world takes for granted. She was gifted this device for ten years, and is now deaf, wearing two cochlear implants.

In late 2021, she founded Ready or Not! Media, a disability awareness strategy firm. "Ready or not?" is a question she is asking all of us. Are you ready to learn more about people with disabilities? Are you ready to rise above the discomfort and become comfortable with the disability community? She is more than ready. She has been preparing for this moment her entire life: to share her commitment and passion, to dismantle the stereotypes, and include people of ALL abilities in the fabric of our workforce and communities.

Visit Ready or Not! Media's website to find out more about Lori's disability awareness strategy consulting firm, and book compelling DEI events for your company today at www.readyornotmedia.com or you can chat with Lori via email lori@readyornotmedia.com. Follow Instagram @readyornotmedia

CONCLUSION

"The world needs more women who are willing to bravely share their stories to inspire and empower other women who are desperately seeking a message of hope and healing."

~ Creative Mannista

Ladies, I hope within each unique story, throughout each page in this book, you're walking away with feelings of joy, inspiration, a new sense of knowledge, love, connection, encouragement, strength, intention, and most importantly, feeling less alone. Remember, we're much stronger when we come together, share our vulnerable, powerful stories, and take off our judgment comparison hats. We're all trying to navigate this world the best we can. Keeping it real—this shit isn't always easy.

No matter what we've been through and continue to go through, we're all created beyond our parents in a vision of love. And through that abundant love, there is feminine energy connecting us. Please close your eyes and feel the connection; it vibrates strong, even in our doubtful moments.

I dated a guy who believed it was okay to punch holes in walls, throw things, break things, and control who I saw and what I did. Yikes! I dated this man because he caught me in a vulnerable state at the time, and to be clear, I freely gave my power to him. He accused me of causing him to act this volatile way. For a long time, even after the relationship ended, I believed him. Almost a year later, I bumped into my Ex and his new girlfriend—they had been together for six months and seemed happy. Like a red scarlet letter stamped on my back screaming, *see, it was you!* But *"The Universe always has our backs,"* as one of my favorite authors and motivational speaker, Gabrielle Bernstein, says.

A few weeks later, through a mutual friend, I found out they weren't happy—or at least his new girlfriend wasn't. My Ex eventually treated her in the same endearing way he treated me—throwing things, breaking things, and trying to control her—until she finally had enough of his BS and also ended the relationship. Although I'd never wish what I went through on another woman, hearing this news stopped the negativity in my brain of self-doubt and constant self-questioning if I was this horrible person my Ex tried to paint me as.

Here's the thing, we all have stuff we need to work on; no one is perfect. For most of us, even in the ideal homes growing up, there are still underlying experiences in our childhood that later mold us in good and challenging ways. Through every adventure, there is a learning lesson that makes us stronger, wiser, and braver. Finding our power from within our experiences and traumas is one of our most significant life lesson practices. Learning and growing from these experiences by releasing negative thoughts and labels is how we ignite the inner love we have within.

Being the lead author of *Miss-Adventures Guide To Ultimate Empowerment For Women,* with all these fantastic co-authors, has been an incredible, life-changing experience that I'm beyond grateful for.

Thank you for reading and, opening your minds and hearts to all the stories—with a few tears, giggles, and cheers—and for enriching and empowering your continued love journey through the stories and practices we have shared.

Xoxo,

Stephanie, aka Miss-Adventures

BEYOND GRATEFUL

I want to thank all my fantastic, incredible, empowering 21 women co-authors who saw my vision and said *YES* to being on my book journey with me—I feel incredibly blessed for every one of you. Thank you for trusting me and this experience, opening your hearts, and sharing your stories. My heart is bursting with so much joy to have you all in my life.

Thank you, Dino Marino, for designing my beautiful book cover and for all your hard work in making my vision a reality.

Thank you, Soo Kim, for my beautiful headshot—you are a gifted photographer—and for being in my life, for your friendship, and for all your support.

A special thank you to one of my co-authors Anna Pereira for your constant check-ins, mentorship, advice, guidance, and listening ear. Most importantly, thank you for your friendship. You are an angel sent from God.

Big shoutout and thank you to my publisher Laura Di Franco, CEO of Brave Healer Productions, and her team for publishing *Miss-Adventures Guide To Ultimate Empowerment For Women*—and making this book collaboration possible, for seeing my vision, and for guiding me in this process. Thank you Laura, for coming into my life, for all your words of wisdom, workshops, marketing, and guidance, and for being incredible, enlightening, and empowering!

Thank you, Karen Sole-Dwyer, Dr. Redd Geurts, Stacey Bourdeau, Valerie Sweeney, and Nancy DeBell Guin, for reminiscing with me so I could share my story with clarity. An extra thank you to Dr. Redd for helping me find Colleen, and to Stacey, for "being nosy" and helping Colleen in her search for me—I am forever grateful for you both.

Thank you, Colleen Ennis, for being the *mom* in my life that God brought to me when I was ready—an additional blessing to my life. Even though you are no longer on this Earth, you are always in my heart space—which is filled with immense joy that I was able to meet, have a relationship with you and be able to share our story with the world.

Thank you, Gwieneverea Duncan-Brandon, Kimberly Malone, Deb DeVigne, Rebecca Swenson, Nancy DeBell Guin, Sonja Motley-Turman, D'Vorah Bailey, Tanya Garner, and Tasha Nix—for all your continual encouragement, love, support, friendship, and belief in me.

Words can't express enough the enormous gratitude I feel for my best friend, Kimberly Malone; thank you for all your guidance, support, a listening ear, for never giving up on me, and for holding me accountable to my *dream goals*—it would have taken me a lot longer to get where I am today without you. I'm immensely grateful for you and the unconditional love and friendship you give me. Love you, lady.

Special thank you to my mother, Mary Roberts-Bailey, for adopting, raising, and being my mom. Thank you for flying to Denver and being my rock when I met Colleen in person for the first time. Through our ups and downs, laughter and tears of navigating each other, I wouldn't have chosen anyone else to have been my mother who raised me. I love you with all my heart, and I'm proud to call you my mother.

I am utterly grateful to my love, partner, and best friend, Damon Miller, for all your patience and understanding so I could immerse in my role as the lead author—I know this wasn't always easy. Thank you for believing in me and never giving up on me—your support, hugs, head rubs, and encouragement have meant a lot. Thank you for being there for me during the stressful moments and knowing how to put a smile on my face. You are my rock, Bae, and I love you more than words can express. Thank you, Bruno and Rocco Miller, for your patience and understanding during this process. I love you both.

Most Importantly, I want to thank God for showing me the direction for *Miss-Adventures Guide to Ultimate Empowerment For Women* and for guiding me in this process. Thank you for bringing all the incredible women authors, my publisher Laura and her team, and the readers reading this book into my life. Thank you for getting me here—as the lead author—I feel grateful, thankful, and blessed every day. Jeremiah 17:7 "blessed is the one who trusts in the LORD, whose confidence is in him."

Love,

Stephanie, aka; Miss-Adventures

ABOUT THE AUTHOR

Stephanie is the CEO of Miss-Adventures, LLC, a Love Expert/Coach and #1 best-selling author whose passion is advising, writing, and empowering women on dating, relationships, break-ups, being successfully happily single, and most importantly, developing genuine self-love. Although the tools for developing love are not easy to obtain—nothing significant in life ever is—the rewards are endless. Her knowledge, experience, and expertise come from her own dating/relationship experiences, extensive self-discovery, and healing, along with her intuitive, empathic skills (given by God as a child). Stephanie finds her experiences help connect to her love clients on a deeper emotional level, which allows them to achieve their personal goals and growth. Stephanie has been a love expert/coach for over 26-plus years with highly successful love results. Her approach is similar to a best friend, who is not afraid to hold one accountable for their actions and be their biggest cheerleader. She creates a judgment-free loving space for her clients and believes life should never be one big apology, but instead, lead by love, forgiveness, understanding, and trust within yourself. Stephanie looks forward to helping empower women on their journey and guiding them on their new adventure to self-love. Please use the QR Code to connect to Stephanie's website—learn more about her, her love coaching, and to contact her.

WHAT WOMEN ARE SAYING ABOUT STEPHANIE/MISS-ADVENTURES

"Stephanie is a super fun, fabulous, and intuitive relationship coach. She not only takes her past experiences to share entertaining and relatable stories but also to break down the lessons and takeaways that could benefit others. Stephanie is an expert in understanding human behavior and communication and, regardless of the outcome, does an extraordinary job of being truthful and honest to deliver wisdom with integrity. Put otherwise, she won't do what you want, but rather what is best for you. Stephanie was instrumental in a couple of my relationships and assisted me in staying true to myself, not ever minimizing my core values, and ultimately to respect myself so that the right man could honor and respect me the same way. She is real and raw but delivers empathy with her candid advice. Honestly. . .the best!"

~ Lauren S., Colorado

"Stephanie Bailey's relationship advice and guidance made a difference in my life. I was devastated when my boyfriend at the time broke up with me during a time when I really needed him. Stephanie spoke from the heart, listened intently, asked questions, and coached me through the process. I reflect back on our discussions and her honest advice. Also, Stephanie is extremely resourceful and recommended articles that she has written, which was great. I would recommend Stephanie for any relationship advice."

~ Gina C., Atlanta, Georgia

"Stephanie has a true desire to share her female power with women everywhere. If you are struggling, she's definitely someone to reach out to for a new prospective."

~ Terri S., Denver, Colorado

"I made my first Love Session with Stephanie in January of 2020. I remember she poured me a cup of tea in a red "love" mug and gave me a red heart to hold. I think I cried for hours after that first session because I finally found someone who understood and knew how to process this journey of love with me. In the first few sessions, we worked a TON on self-love. What I learned was: All love starts with me. I worked for months and months on self-love. We later moved to my romantic relationship, friendships, and family relationships. After years of internet dating and living in "Menver," I wanted to do things differently. In March of 2021, my boyfriend proposed, and in November of 2021, we got married. I still meet with Stephanie regularly to continue the hard work. She is the type of coach who allows you to interview for a new job mid-session while bringing a bottle of champagne for you to take home. Stephanie is loving, kind, and real. She taught me how to focus on myself and my husband instead of trying to please the world. I am a people pleaser, so working with her has been life-changing. My husband and I are now starting IVF. While I have an IVF support group, I can't imagine starting this without Stephanie. I know becoming a mother is going to take a lot of self-love and acceptance, and that is where we started. My time with Stephanie has been full circle, and I would recommend anyone and every one take time to work with her."

~ Jodi D., Denver, Colorado

"In my three years of experience discussing relationship dynamics with Stephanie Bailey, I have found her to have deep, insightful advice that can only be gotten through experience. She has taken her experience and turned it into wisdom all women should share."

~ EJ Yoder, Ph.D., Colorado

"I wanted to write a note about Miss-adventure. She is not only a wonderful friend to me but has been there for me through several of my relationships. As someone that isn't familiar with a lesbian relationship herself, all her advice has been spot on. So regardless of your love relationship, Stephanie knows all the dynamics of two people coming together and finding out how to love themselves and to be ready for long-lasting real love. Thank you."

~ Krystal Brown, New Mexico

"What I appreciate most about Stephanie is her unconditional dedication and passion for invigorating those around her. Stephanie has supported me in some of the most difficult times of my life, both physically and emotionally. Her expertise as a massage therapist highlights her intuitive healing powers. Her Eastern and Western approaches have provided me with the tools to rebuild and improve my daily life. Stephanie's down-to-earth, authentic personality has been equally represented in her work as an author."

~ Dr. Dana Waldbaum, Colorado

"My life in dating has been one filled with lots of happiness and joy as well as misunderstandings and lows. Upon meeting Stephanie and listening to her advice, I began to realize that one of my areas of improvement was staying true to myself and my voice. I realized that goal setting and sticking to it in love was as important as a goal at work. Keep your promises to yourself. Her wisdom and strong sense of self are welcome. Stephanie has the ability to see through the BS and call out the areas that need attention. She is a strong individual that cares about women and wants what's best for love and acceptance for yourself and in love."

~ Stephanie V., Colorado

"When situations happen in dating, relationships, and well just life, most of us have the tendency to think we are unique and the only one this has happened to. Through Stephanie's writing and coaching, she is able to reach women in a way that is connective, inspiring, and empowering. Stephanie is truly making the world a better place, one conversation at a time."

~ Kimberly M., California

"What can I say. . .if you want the real deal on anything, Stephanie is your go-to girl! She will give it to you straight no matter what the issue. Real talk, from a real woman. . .She DOESN'T disappoint! She's an added bonus to anyone's life."

~ Jennifer Jankowski, Denver, Colorado

"Miss-Adventures is a light-hearted approach offering smart, sometimes sassy, no-nonsense advice for the dating world and beyond. All topics embrace self-love and encourage self-exploration to achieve a well-balanced life. Stephanie's positive energy and helpful personality shine bright and can't help but make you feel you are not alone in your journey with relationships and, more importantly, learning to embrace your inner strength while practicing daily gratitude."

~ Dr. Robin Asbury, Colorado

"When it comes to relationships, Stephanie is the best. I've been married for over 20 years, and no relationship is perfect. When I have a bump in the road, I talk to her about it, and she gives me the best advice. Stephanie listens and analyzes the situation and always gets me back on track feeling good and confident about my decisions. Thank you, Stephanie, for being a great friend and always being there when I need you. Love you, lady!"

~ Deb G., Colorado

"The combination of Stephanie's wisdom and confidence abound. She provides support in ways that are invaluable and pushes you in just the right ways. She leads with love and kindness. I am grateful for all her direct and indirect advice she has given me over the years."

~ Annie K., Colorado

"Stephanie, you have helped me in so many ways I don't know if I could ever repay you. Not only do I know my worth, but I've learned to be patient; what is for me will be for me. After my long-term breakup, I was down, and with your advice, I was able to see that the grass is greener on the other side. . .there is hope, and there will always be God by my side who will never forsake me. Thank you for reminding me that I am a beautiful person inside and out. I will forever be grateful to God for leading the way and to you for walking into my life when I needed it the most."

~ Cris U., Colorado

"Stephanie is an exceptional valuable expert on relationship advice. Over the years, her wisdom and guidance have been at the core of my personal growth on my journey. xoxoxo Love you!"

~ Nancy G., RN BSN, Colorado

"Stephanie, Miss Adventures, has been a relationship guide ever since high school. She was always my sounding board for relationship advice because as most of us know, teenage love can be oh so complicated. Even now, as an adult and married for nearly 20 years, I find her articles to be relatable and honest. Her desire to assist single women, and women in general, as they go through their relationships has allowed her to create her platform, and through coaching, print, radio, and digital media she is reaching the masses and making a difference. When a woman hits a tough patch in her relationship, it is important for her to hear a sound, non-judgmental voice of reason, and Stephanie is that voice."

~ Dr. Gwieneverea Brandon, Texas

Made in the USA
Middletown, DE
17 October 2022

12881674R00128